2ⁿᵈ edition

masterMind

Workbook

Mike Boyle

Anna Osborn

Concept development:
Mariela Gil Vierma

Level 1

Macmillan Education
4 Crinan Street
London N1 9XW
A division of Macmillan Publishers Limited

Companies and representatives throughout the world

ISBN 9780230469723 with key
ISBN 9780230469730 without key

This edition published 2015
First edition published 2010

Designed by emc design limited
Illustrated by Sally Elford p55
Cover design by Tony Richardson, Wooden Ark Ltd.
Cover photograph courtesy of Getty Images/Zero Creatives

Picture research by Victoria Gaunt

The authors would like to thank the schools, teachers, and students
whose input has been invaluable in preparing this new edition. They
would also like to thank the editorial and design teams at Macmillan for
doing such a great job of organizing the material and bringing it to life.

The publishers would like to thank the following educators and
institutions who reviewed materials and provided us with invaluable
insight and feedback for the development of masterMind 2nd edition:

Isidro Almedarez, Deniz Atesok, Monica Delgadillo, Elaine Hodgson,
Mark Lloyd, Rufus Vaughan-Spruce, Kristof van Houdt, Rob Duncan,
James Conboy, Jonathan Danby, Fiona Craig, Martin Guilfoyle, Rodrigo
Rosa

The authors and publishers would like to thank the following for
permission to reproduce the following material:

Extract from 'Winston Churchill didn't really exist say teens' by Aislinn
Simpson © Telegraph Group Limited 2008, first published in the Daily
Telegraph 4 February 2008. Reprinted by permission of the publisher.
www.telegraph.co.uk
Extract from 'What's frying at Walkie Scorchie?' by Harry Wallop ©
Telegraph Group Limited 2013, first published in the Daily Telegraph
3 September 2013. Reprinted by permission of the publisher.
www.telegraph.co.uk, Material adapted from 'Water Footprints'
published on the Water Footprint Network, www.waterfootprint.org,
Material adapted from 'The Science of Competition' by Kara Miller &
Kinnie ChapinFirst published by WGBH News as a part of the WGBH
Innovation hub http://blogs.wgbh.org/innovation-hub/, Material adapted
from 'Real to Me: Girls and Reality TV' ©2011 Girl Scouts of the USA.
Adapted for educational use. www.girlscouts.org, Extract from 'Nurture
Shock Why everything we think about raising our children is wrong' by
Po Bronson and Ashley Merryman © Po Bronson and Ashley Merryman
2011. Published by Ebury Press. Reprinted with permission of the
Random House Group and Curtis Brown Ltd, Material adapted from
'Selfie City' Reprinted with permission. http://selfiecity.net/, Extract
from 'The death of photography: are camera phones destroying an
artform?' by Stuart Jeffries © Guardian News & Media Ltd 2013.
First published in the Guardian 13 December 2013. Reprinted with
permission. www.theguardian.com, Extract adapted from 'The Five Lost
Cities of the Future'. First published on Scribol. Used with permission.
www.scribol.com, Material from 'Athletes fight back over McDonald's
Games ads' by Simon Chapman, originally published by Crikey on 15th
August 2008. Used with permission. http://www.crikey.com.au/

The authors and publishers would like to thank the following for
permission to reproduce their photographs:

Alamy/David Bleeker Photography p30(b), **Alamy**/billdayone p35(t),
Alamy/Blend Images pp57, 69, Alamy/Cultura Creative p6(t), Alamy/
Phil Degginger p74(b), Alamy/Lev Dolgachov p11, Alamy/Hero Images
Inc. p22, Alamy/Huntstock, Inc p54, Alamy/Fredrick Kippe p19, Alamy/
Dan Leeth p29(b), Alamy/Christian Musat p74(a-bear), Alamy/Susan &
Allan Parker p58, Alamy/Image Source Plus p48, Alamy/epa european
pressphoto agency b.v. p38(d), Alamy/Radius Images p8, Alamy/Jack
Sullivan p31(b), Alamy/Purcell Team p29(t), Alamy/John Warburton-
Lee p15, Alamy/Westend61 GmbH p18, Alamy/Matthew Williams-Ellis
p24; Bananastock p26(bc); **Bridgeman Images**/Jamestown, Virginia,
1607 (engraving), English School, (17th century) / Private Collection/
Peter Newark American Pictures p72; **Corbis** p34, Corbis/ Paul Burns/
Blend Images p61, Corbis/ umar87/Demotix/Demotix p60, Corbis/
Patrik Giardino p40, Corbis/ALEX GRIMM/Reuters p52, Corbis/David
Harrigan/ableimages p25, Corbis/KidStock/Blend Images p50(b),
Corbis/Inti St Clair/Blend Images pp10(3), 16(t), Corbis/John Lamm/
Transtock p43(t), Corbis/Tomas Rodriguez p31(t), Corbis/Wavebreak
Media LTD/Wavebreak Media Ltd p46, Corbis/237/Chris Ryan/Ocean
p36(b), Corbis/68/Ocean p53, Corbis/Atlantide Phototravel p44, Corbis/
andy Olson/National Geographic Society p51, Corbis/John Lund/
Marc Romanelli/Blend Images p27, Corbis/ Vladimir Serov/Blend
Images p65(tr), Corbis/Yevgen Timashov/beyond p65(tl); **EyeWire**/
Getty Images p56; **Getty Images** pp26(t), 35(b), Getty Images/
AFP/Staff p74(d), Getty Images/AFP/Stringer p38(b), Getty Images/
andresr p70, Getty Images/Brand New Images p5(c), Getty Images/
Anna Bryukhanova p30(t), Getty Images/Carlo A p4, Getty Images/
Nick David p67(a), Getty Images/Cesare Ferrari p68, Getty Images/
ilbusca p59, Getty Images/Andrew Ilyasov p62(t), Getty Images/Daniel
Ingold p65(cr), Getty Images/Inti St Clair p14, Getty Images/Christian
Kober p38(a), Getty Images/Lambert p20, Getty Images/Bertrand Linet
p38(c), Getty Images/Diane Levit/Design Pics p28(t), Getty Images/ain
Masterton p29(c), Getty Images/Zoran Milich p67(b), Getty Images/
Erin Patrice O'Brien p6(b), Getty Images/WPA Pool/Pool p42, Getty
Images/Eric Gregory Powell p28(b), Getty Images/VikramRaghuvanshi
p7(b), Getty Images/Radius Images p26(tc), Getty Images/Eric Raptosh
Photography p7(t), Getty Images/David Ramos/Stringe p38(e), Getty
Images/Gregor Schuster p12, Getty Images/Westend61 p10(2), Getty
Images/XiXinXing p64(tl); Glow Images p10(4); **ImageSource** pp10(1),
16(b); **Photodisc** p74(c); **Press Association Image**/Andy Scofield/
PA Archives pp45(background, insert), Press Association Images/
KAREL PRINSLOO/AP p50(t); **Rex Features**/Zuma p73; **Superstock**/
Beyond p43(b); **Thinkstock** p13, 26(b), Thinkstock/BananaStock p49,
Thinkstock/istock pp5(t,b), 17(l), 23, 36(t), 63, 64(b,tr), 75, Thinkstock/
Stockbyte p17(r), Thinkstock/TongRo Images p32.

Printed and bound in Thailand

2018   2017   2016   2015
10 9 8 7 6 5 4 3 2 1

CONTENTS

AUDIO SCRIPT

UNIT 1 WHO DO YOU THINK YOU ARE?

1 READING: for different purposes

1 FUTURE IDENTITIES: Changing identities in the next ten years

EXECUTIVE SUMMARY

Identity is changing. Over the next ten years, people's identities are likely to be significantly affected by hyper-connectivity (where people can be constantly connected online), the spread of social media, and the increase in online personal information.

What does identity mean today?

- **PEOPLE HAVE MANY OVERLAPPING IDENTITIES**
  This report considers several aspects of identities including country, religion, family background, and social status. A person can have all of these identities at the same time. For example, at home a person may find their identity as a parent most important, while at work they might identify most as an employee. Online, their sense of identity may be connected to a hobby.

- **PEOPLE EXPRESS THEIR IDENTITIES IN DIFFERENT WAYS**
  On the internet, it is easier for people to adopt an identity that is different from the way in which others stereotype them. Some people even feel that they have achieved their "true" identity for the first time online. For example, some people may socialize more successfully, and express themselves more freely, online. This is one of the ways in which online identities can transform offline identities.

- **IDENTITIES HAVE VALUE**
  People's identities have personal, social, and commercial value. As more personal data is stored online, there is the potential for positive social interaction, but also for criminal exploitation or misuse.

Information source: http://www.bis.gov.uk

2 EXPRESSING (AND PROTECTING!) YOUR ONLINE IDENTITY

MARK: Is it a good idea for young people to be on social media?

LIZ: Yes and no. You can find people who have similar interests, and you can express who you really are, with pictures, blogs, and more.

MARK: Those are the good things. What is the downside?

LIZ: Well, we all change over time, but this is particularly true for young people; you're not the same person at 20 as you were at 15. That can be a problem because things you put online now may be embarrassing in a few years.

MARK: Are there other dangers?

LIZ: Yes. Young people need to remember that we have multiple identities. You may see yourself as a future pop star, for example, but you're also a student, an employee, and a brother or sister or family member. It's very easy for the wrong person to see something. For example, if you complain about your teachers online, the college you want to go to might see that, and it doesn't look good.

MARK: What about bullying?

LIZ: It's a real risk for young people. It's harder to control your identity online because anyone can post information about you. People can say hurtful and untrue things about you. But overall, I think social media is a great thing for young people if it's used carefully.

A Look quickly at the two texts. Then answer the questions.

1 Where is each text from? Write the letter of the source next to each text number.

Text 1 _____ Text 2 _____

a) a magazine article
b) a textbook
c) a novel
d) a government report

2 Why would we read each text? Write the letter of the reason next to each text number. There may be more than one reason for each text.

Text 1 _____ Text 2 _____

a) for pleasure
b) for information
c) to find out opinions
d) to find out news

B Read the texts in Exercise A again. Choose T (true) or F (false) for each statement.

1 Technology hasn't changed identity in the last ten years.	T / F
2 Most people have the same identity in all situations.	T / F
3 Some people find it easier to express their true identity online.	T / F
4 Your identity can be worth money to some people.	T / F
5 Only you can change and control your online identity.	T / F
6 People need to think about who might see their information online.	T / F

2 VOCABULARY: personal identity

A Choose the correct options to complete the article.

We ask, you answer!

Today's question:
What influences your identity?

MATT, 41 | ● click to listen

Wow, that's a tough question! I think when I was younger, my friends really shaped who I was, so the **(1)** *social status / social group* I was part of was very important. Also I had a lot of big **(2)** *life goals / family values* back then. I wanted to be a musician, so music was my life and really influenced my identity. But things are different now. I'm a husband, and I'm a dad—that's how I see myself. So I guess **(3)** *family values / family background* are more important to my sense of identity now.

YASMIN, 20 | ● click to listen

Well, I've thought a lot about this since I came to the U.S. for college. In the middle east, where I come from, a lot of people get a **(4)** *value / sense* of identity from their **(5)** *family background / life goals*. Not just your parents, but your grandparents and even great-grandparents show people who you are. If you come from a "good" family, your **(6)** *social group / social status* is higher and people treat you better. Now, I still think family is a really important factor in your identity, but it's not the only thing. The subject you study, your friends, and interests are factors, too.

B 🎧 01 Listen and check your answers.

3 COMMUNICATION STRATEGY: agreeing and disagreeing

A 🎧 **02** Listen to a debate on a radio show. Check which person makes each point below.

		Mark Owens	Lisa Adams
1	It is good to buy cool clothes for children.	☐	☐
2	Children need to be part of a social group.	☐	☐
3	Children need comfortable clothes, not designer clothes.	☐	☐
4	Children should be allowed to look good if they want to.	☐	☐
5	Many parents can't afford to buy designer clothes for their children.	☐	☐
6	Personality, not clothes, helps develop a child's sense of identity.	☐	☐

B Listen again. Put the phrases for agreeing and disagreeing in the order that you hear them (1–6).

____ I couldn't agree more.

____ Yes and no.

____ In a sense, you're right.

____ Well, yes, to a certain extent, but …

____ I'm sorry, but I just don't think that's true.

____ I'm afraid I can't agree.

4 GRAMMAR: review of past tenses

A Check the sentences that refer to actions or states in progress in the past.

1 ☐ Kim was studying in Europe during the winter break.
2 ☐ Fareed had read the book before he saw the movie.
3 ☐ Don't worry, Marisol. We weren't talking about you.
4 ☐ Mia did prepare for the interview, but it wasn't enough.

WATCH OUT!

✗ I was having to wear a uniform when I was in school.

✓ _____

B Choose the correct options to complete the comments.

LUISA POSTED A PICTURE

This was me at my big quinceañera (15th birthday party). Look at what I **(1)** *was wearing / had worn*! They say the quinceañera is when you become an adult. Ha ha!

JACOB:
I think you look nice! I **(2)** *wasn't having / didn't have* a big party for my 15th, but I **(3)** *did had / did have* a big one for my 16th. I **(4)** *didn't look like / wasn't looking like* an adult, either.

NATALIA:
Ha ha, you should see my quinceañera pictures. I **(5)** *was never wearing / had never worn* makeup before that day, so I **(6)** *put on / did put on* way too much. I really **(7)** *did feel / had felt* grown-up, though!

5 VOCABULARY: *sense*

A Look at the words and phrases in bold in the sentences. Write N (noun),
V (verb), or A (adjective).

1 ___ Maria said the book changed her life, but I found it confusing and couldn't **make sense of** it.
2 ___ My friends always **sense** when I'm feeling low.
3 ___ No one was surprised that Tom wore shorts when it was so cold. He doesn't have any **common sense**.
4 ___ I've always been a **sensitive** person and try to understand how other people are feeling.
5 ___ Instead of being **sensible** and studying business, Louise took classes in art and philosophy.
6 ___ Don't ask Diego about his family. They don't get along, so it's a **sensitive** topic.
7 ___ Sophia's best quality is her **sense of humor**. She can always make people laugh.

B Complete this magazine excerpt with the correct form of the words and
phrases in bold from Exercise A.

My many identities
posted by Daniel
3 days ago

I've been reading a government report on the future of identity. It's fascinating, although some parts
are a bit technical and it's difficult to **(1)** _____ them. According to the report, no
one has just one identity. We all have different identities in different situations. Here are a few of mine!

- At college: I'm Daniel the class clown. People say I have a great **(2)** _____ and
  everyone loves my jokes—well, except for the teachers!
- At work: I'm an intern at a big company and I want a job there after graduation. People there
  see my **(3)** _____ side—I always find reasonable, practical solutions to
  problems. My boss says I'm the only one there who has any **(4)** _____.
- With my friends, I'm known as a **(5)** _____ person who listens well and gives
  good advice. I can **(6)** _____ when my friends are upset, and I'm always there
  for them. My friends can talk to me about anything. No topic is too **(7)** _____!

6 GRAMMAR: *would, used to, be + always + –ing*

WATCH OUT!
(X) I always was taking pictures to
express myself.

(✓) _____

A Look at the structures. Write *PP* if the structure is
used to talk about the present or past, and *P* if it's used
to talk about the past only.

1 ___ *would (always/never)* + base form
2 ___ *(always/never) used to* + base form
3 ___ *be always + –ing* form

B Rewrite Nicole's comments using the structure in parentheses.

"When I was young, **(1)** I tried to be part of the 'cool' group. **(2)** I did what my friends
told me to do, and **(3)** I often behaved irresponsibly. **(4)** I didn't
have a strong sense of my own identity and, as a result, **(5)** I didn't feel confident."

1 (*used to*)   *I used to try to be part of the 'cool' group.*
2 (*would/always*)   _____
3 (*be/always*)   _____
4 (*never/used to*) _____
5 (*would/never*)   _____

C Complete the story with the correct form of the phrases from
the box. You can use some phrases more than once and, in some
cases, more than one answer is possible.

| always do   always make sure   never help   never take   work |

"It's funny how things change. I remember how, when I was really young, my father **(1)** _____
away from home a lot. Because of this, he **(2)** _____ my mom in the house or play with us. In
contrast, my mom was the typical responsible wife and mother. She **(3)** _____ housework, and
she **(4)** _____ we had what we needed. She **(5)** _____ time off or relax. But nowadays,
Dad works nearby, so he stays home while she goes out and has fun. It's great!"

skillsStudio

A Read the text quickly. Then choose the correct option to complete the statements.

1   According to the text, *there is one / there are many* possible definitions of the word "identity."

2   The text says that a person can have *only one / more than one* identity, depending on the situation.

3   Everyone has *three / one of three* main types of identity, according to the text.

B Read the text again and choose the correct sentence for each blank. There is one extra sentence that you do not need to use.

A   These include identities such as family relationships, friendships, membership of communities, and attachment to particular places.

B   There are several reasons why identities are important for policy makers in government.

C   They can be also *exclusive*, defined by *not* being a member of a particular group.

D   However, others have the potential to change over time, or may remain the same (such as national identity or attachment to places where people live or work).

E   These can be used to verify that people are who they say they are.

F   There is, therefore, no single definition of "identity" that everyone agrees upon.

C Read the text again and answer these questions.

1   In the second paragraph, what is the main point about identities?
   a)   Your identity is created and controlled mostly by other people.
   b)   Every identity is unique and no two people have the same one.
   c)   The main way identities are formed is by rejection from a social group.
   d)   Identities have many parts and are formed in many different ways.

2   The word *rejection* in line 31 means …
   a)   a feeling of sadness.
   b)   including.
   c)   refusal to accept.
   d)   the choice to quit something.

3   Which of the following is an example of social identity?
   a)   being on a soccer team
   b)   having blond hair and blue eyes
   c)   earning a good salary
   d)   having a college degree

4   The word *distinct* in line 58 means …
   a)   obvious.
   b)   separate and different.
   c)   easily seen or heard.
   d)   excellent.

5   Having parents who are immigrants from another country is an example of …
   a)   social identity.
   b)   biographical identity.
   c)   biometric identity.
   d)   none of these.

6   In the last paragraph, what is the main point about identities?
   a)   The parts of a person's identity can change over time.
   b)   Friendship groups change more easily than gender or ethnicity.
   c)   A person's family roles are not the same thing as his or her identity.
   d)   Hobbies are an important part of many people's identities.

D You are applying for a study-abroad program. As part of the application process, write an essay of about 200 words on the following topic: "My personal identity: past, present, and future."

2.1 Definition of identity

1 A person's "identity" can be defined as those characteristics that determine who a person is. This includes a person's perception of themselves as similar to, or different from, other people, but identities can also be imposed by others.

5 Dictionary definitions of "identity" are often based on a very simplistic notion of identity made popular during the 1950s by the developmental psychologist Erik Erikson. His concept suggested that identity is shaped by the interaction of three elements: a person's biological characteristics,

10 their psychology, and their cultural context. Since then, however, identity has become a key concept in a wide range of academic subjects, including political science, the social sciences, and the humanities, and definitions of identity have expanded as a result. **(1)** ___

15 These different interpretations have shown that identities are socially constructed and highly complex. Many different types of identity are now discussed, such as cultural identity, organizational identity, and national identity. Even for an individual, there are many possible identities that overlap

20 and can change over time or in different circumstances. People, therefore, each have an identity that combines many different aspects about themselves, and together these give them a sense of meaning in their lives.

Identities can be *elective* or chosen by a person, such as

25 by membership of a social group. They can also be *ascribed* or decided and controlled by others, for example, through data about a person collected by a supermarket. Identities can be *inclusive*, such as membership of a family, team, religion, or other group. **(2)** ___ Again, these identities can

30 be controlled by the individual or by others, for instance, through rejection from a group.

In general, there are three overlapping types of identities: social, biographical, and biometric:

- SOCIAL IDENTITIES are generated through roles
35 and relationships between people, and wider culture and society. **(3)** ___

- BIOGRAPHICAL IDENTITIES are identities that individuals might use to describe themselves to another or how they perceive themselves. These might include

40 national identity, as well as ethnicity and religion— although these also have a strong social role. Identities such as a professional role or financial status might also be considered biographical identities.

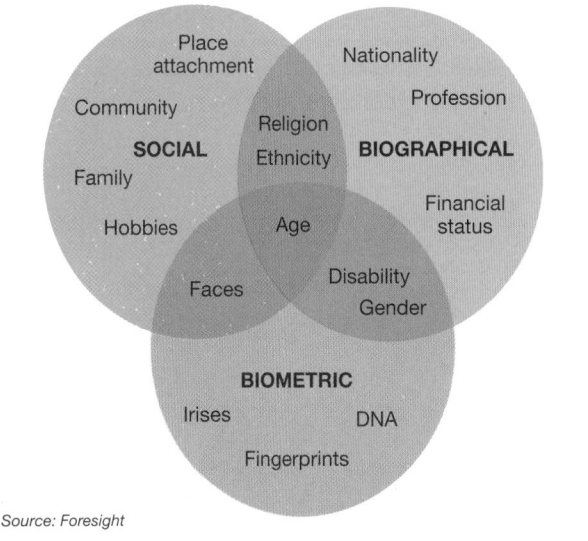

Fig.2.1: Types of identities: social, biographical, and biometric identities, and some examples of each type.

Source: Foresight

- BIOMETRIC IDENTITIES are those aspects of identity related to the body, including unique
45 characteristics such as DNA, fingerprints, irises, and faces. **(4)** ___

A person therefore has a sense of self that is constructed from many elements, and these could be considered as

50 different "identities." Some aspects of an individual's identity are unlikely to change (gender, disability, or ethnicity). Some types of identity change only very gradually over a person's lifetime (for example, age). **(5)** ___ Other social identities can change more easily, for example, when

55 people belong to different communities (including online communities), or friendship groups. Some stages of life carry shifting family roles and responsibilities that create distinct identities, for example, being a child, being in a relationship, becoming a parent or grandparent, while

60 professional and financial identities can change as jobs, status, careers, and experiences alter. People can also have identities related to hobbies, leisure, and consumption, which for some people can change rapidly, while others maintain their "hobbies" as an important part of themselves over a long period of time.

UNIT 2 GLOBAL VIEWS

1 LISTENING: understanding discourse markers

A 🔊 **03** Listen to four people describing their experiences of globalization. Complete the sentences with the words from the box.

> communications   the economy   the service industry   trade

1 Speaker 1 is discussing _____.
2 Speaker 2 is talking about _____.
3 Speaker 3 is concerned about _____.
4 Speaker 4 is describing _____.

B 🔊 **04** Listen to speakers 1–3 again. Write the letters of the discourse markers (a–e) that each speaker uses.

Speaker 1 ___ ___ ___
Speaker 2 ___ ___ ___
Speaker 3 ___ ___ ___

a) like   **b)** kind of   **c)** well   **d)** you know   **e)** I mean

C 🔊 **05** Listen to Speaker 4 again. Complete the text with the discourse markers from Exercise B.

I think globalization's cool. I love using social networking sites because,
(1) _____, it **(2)** _____ means that I have friends all over the world now.
I have, **(3)** _____, 500 friends. It's awesome. **(4)** _____, they send me
pictures, music, videos—all kinds of stuff from their countries—and, **(5)** _____,
I send them things from my country, too. It's amazing.

2 VOCABULARY: globalization

A Match the words or phrases (1–6) with their definitions (a–f).

1 economic growth (*n.*)   **a)** relating to a particular geographic area
2 profits (*n.*)   **b)** financial gains
3 multinational (*adj.*)   **c)** be in control of
4 regional (*adj.*)   **d)** an increase in the size of the economy
5 facilitate (*v.*)   **e)** make something easier
6 dominate (*v.*)   **f)** relating to more than two countries

B Choose the correct options to complete the sentences.

1 The company is *multinational* / *regional* with offices all around the United States, throughout Latin America, and in Australia.
2 Globalization has been good for the whole country because there's been *economic growth* / *profits*, which has led to a decrease in unemployment.
3 Large corporations *facilitate* / *dominate* the market, which means that small companies struggle to survive.
4 The company announced that they had made *economic growth* / *profits* of $3 million.
5 Right now, we only have a few *multinational* / *regional* offices in and around Denver, but we're looking to expand into new areas next year.
6 Globalization *facilitates* / *dominates* communication because it has become so much easier to talk to people on the other side of the world.

3 GRAMMAR: verbs with stative and dynamic uses

A Complete the sentences with the correct form of the verb in parentheses.

1 I _____ (have) friends, family, and colleagues around the world.
2 What time _____ (see) your parents?
3 I _____ (think) our city is losing its identity.
4 Multinational companies _____ (be) the largest employers in the city.

B This comment contains five mistakes with stative and dynamic verbs. Cross out the mistakes and write the correct form.

 LOVE ACROSS THE GLOBE

My girlfriend and I had seen each other for three years when her company offered her a job in the Shanghai office. It was being an amazing opportunity, so she moved there last September, and we're not seeing each other very often. It isn't being ideal, but there are a lot of ways to keep in touch. And we've just gotten engaged, so I'm thinking that old saying, "absence makes the heart grow fonder," might just be true!

WATCH OUT!

Ⓧ I think of applying for a transfer to the Mexico City office next year.

✓ _____
_____

4 GRAMMAR: repeated and double comparatives

A Match (1–6) with (a–f) to make complete sentences.

1 The more competition there is,
2 With new technology we can
3 More and more old people are
4 The more we write text messages,
5 Thanks to DVDs, fewer and fewer
6 The more I use my cell phone,

a) starting to use social networking sites.
b) the worse our spelling becomes.
c) the cheaper smartphones are becoming.
d) the more I depend on it.
e) upload music faster and faster.
f) people go to the movies now.

B Decide which sentences in Exercise A are repeated comparatives and which are double comparatives. Write the sentence numbers in the blanks.

a) Repeated comparatives ___ ___ ___
b) Double comparatives ___ ___ ___

C Choose the correct options to complete the blog.

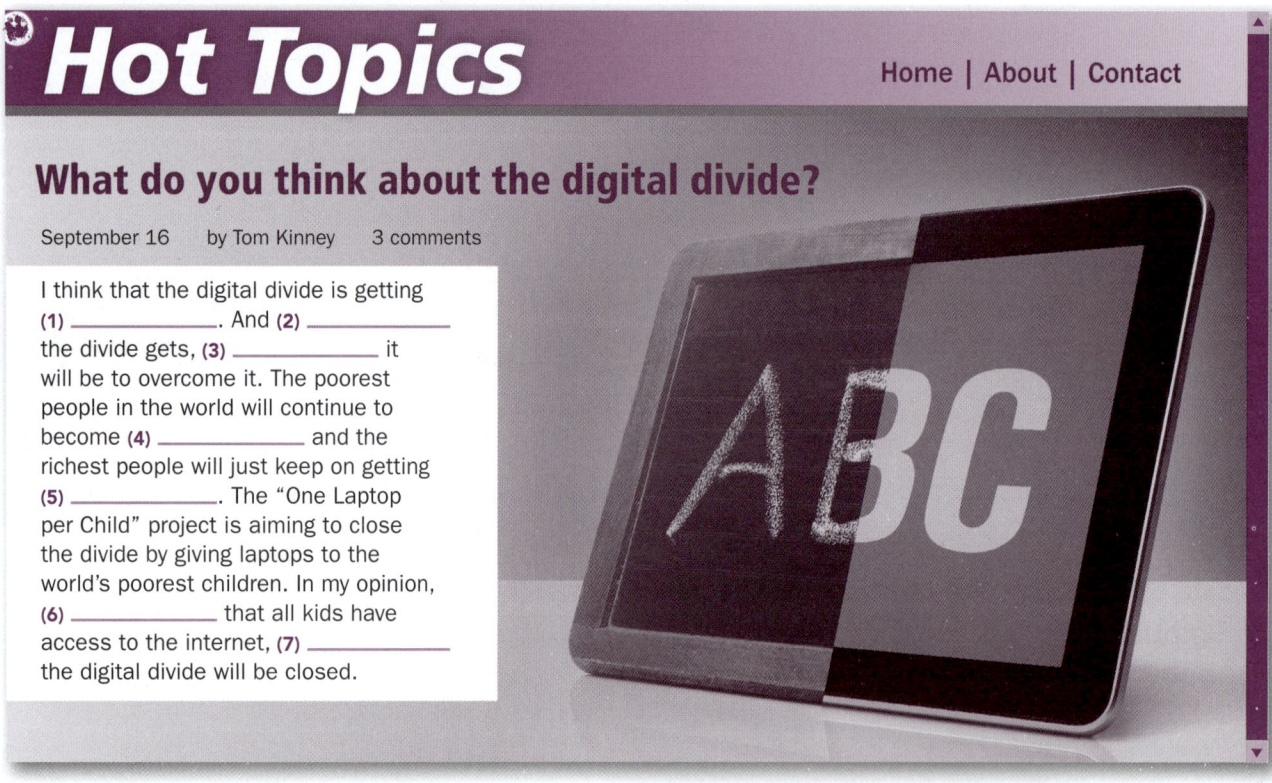

Hot Topics

Home | About | Contact

What do you think about the digital divide?

September 16   by Tom Kinney   3 comments

I think that the digital divide is getting (1) _____. And (2) _____ the divide gets, (3) _____ it will be to overcome it. The poorest people in the world will continue to become (4) _____ and the richest people will just keep on getting (5) _____. The "One Laptop per Child" project is aiming to close the divide by giving laptops to the world's poorest children. In my opinion, (6) _____ that all kids have access to the internet, (7) _____ the digital divide will be closed.

1 a) worse and worse   b) the worse
2 a) bigger and bigger   b) the bigger
3 a) harder and harder   b) the harder
4 a) poorer and poorer   b) the poorer
5 a) richer and richer   b) the richer
6 a) sooner and sooner   b) the sooner
7 a) faster and faster   b) the faster

WATCH OUT!

✗ Multinational companies are becoming more dominant and more dominant.

✓ _____
_____
_____

5 VOCABULARY: verbs for taking social action

A 🔊 06 Listen and write the words you hear.

1 _____ 3 _____ 5 _____ 7 _____
2 _____ 4 _____ 6 _____ 8 _____

B **Choose the correct option to complete the sentences.**

1 Thousands of people _____ in a demonstration yesterday against globalization.
   a) participated   b) generated   c) sustained

2 We must shop locally in order to _____ small businesses.
   a) value   b) sustain   c) campaign

3 Multinational companies _____ a lot of employment worldwide.
   a) campaign   b) generate   c) participate

4 It's worth paying a little bit more for products in order to _____ the local economy.
   a) generate   b) value   c) support

5 Globalization _____ free trade between countries.
   a) campaigns   b) participates   c) promotes

6 The weekly farmers' market has really _____ the local economy.
   a) boosted   b) valued   c) participated

7 If we _____ small local stores, then we should spend money there, instead of shopping online.
   a) generate   b) value   c) boost

8 The politician _____ for the trade ban to be lifted.
   a) participated   b) generated   c) campaigned

6 WRITING: a formal email

A **Read this email and choose the correct formal expressions.**

> **To:** Miguel Godoy   **From:** ksteinmann@globe4u.com
> **Subject:** Globe4U
>
> **(1)** *Hi Miguel! / Dear Mr. Godoy,*
> **(2)** *Thanks so much for applying for / Thank you for your interest in* a summer vacation job with Globe4U. There are still opportunities to work in Haiti in June and August.
> **(3)** *Just tell me / Could you let me know* which month you would prefer?
> **(4)** *You will be required to attend / You have to come to* a meeting with me in order to discuss what the work involves. There are two possible dates for this: May 5 at 10 a.m., or May 14 at 3 p.m. Please let me know which is more convenient for you.
> **(5)** *See you at the meeting / I look forward to meeting you.*
> **(6)** *With love, / Regards,*
> **(7)** *Klaus Steinmann, Director, Globe4U / Klaus*

B **This formal email contains six mistakes. Underline the mistakes and rewrite the email correctly in your notebook using language from Exercise A.**

> Hi Klaus!
> Thanks so much for your email.
> I would prefer to work in June rather than August, and I'm available to come in to discuss the work on May 5 at 10 a.m. Just tell me if there's any preparation that I can do for the meeting?
> See you then.
> With love,
> Miguel

skillsStudio

A Read the book review and answer the question.

Review ▶ **Sustainable Travel** Scott Williams $19.99

An exciting new book by best-selling author Scott Williams, Sustainable Travel, is perfect for adventurous travelers with a conscience. Based on his personal experiences, the author explains how we can get the most authentic experience of different cultures while ensuring that we don't harm the environment. He also explains to us how we can make certain that the money we spend ends up in the pockets of the communities we visit, rather than going to multinational tour operators.

The reviewer thinks that the main function of this book is to explain to readers how to …

a) experience different cultures.
b) have a conscience.
c) have interesting and ethical vacations.

B 🎧 07 Listen to the radio interview. Number the topics in the order that you hear them discussed.

☐ the harm that tourism can do the environment
☐ what ethical tourism is
☐ how to be an ethical tourist
☐ the harm that tourism can do to local communities

C Listen to the radio interview again, and complete the mind map.

(1) _____

(2) _____

How can tourism harm the environment?

(1) _____

(3) _____

Scott's radio interview

How can tourism harm local communities?

(1) _____

(2) _____

How can we become ethical tourists?

(2) _____

(3) _____

D Listen to the radio interview again. Match the phrases (1–6) with their correct meanings (a–f).

1	positive/negative impact	a)	materials provided by nature, such as water, that can be used by humans
2	carbon emissions	b)	good/bad effect
3	natural resources	c)	gases released into the air when we burn fossil fuels
4	tourism developments	d)	when more materials are used to wrap something than is necessary
5	excess packaging	e)	places where you can dispose of trash
6	waste facilities	f)	areas that are built up for use by visitors

E Listen to the radio interview again and answer these questions.

1 An ethical tourist has ———————— on any place they visit.
  a) a positive rather than negative impact
  b) a negative rather than positive impact
  c) no impact at all

2 Scott says that every day there are about ———————— airplane flights worldwide.
  a) 9,300
  b) 93,000
  c) 930,000

3 Tourists destroy natural habitats by …
  a) littering.
  b) playing golf.
  c) flying on airplanes.

4 Scott mentions the golf course to show how tourism can …
  a) destroy some of the world's most beautiful, remote areas.
  b) use up a lot of the natural resources in an area.
  c) create jobs in an area.

5 John suggests that it's unrealistic to expect tourists …
  a) not to travel by plane.
  b) to leave excess packaging at home.
  c) to ask about the ethics of their tour operator.

F Write an opinion essay of about 250 words in your notebook on the following statement: "Every traveler should have a positive impact on all the places they visit."

UNIT 3 FAME AND FORTUNE

1 GRAMMAR: reported speech — verbs and past perfect

A Complete the sentences with the correct form of the verbs in parentheses.

1 Oscar told us we _had to wait_ (*must wait*) behind the rope to get the singer's autograph.
2 Linda explained that she _____ (*never try*) to get a celebrity's autograph before.
3 Ethan said that he _____ (*can't believe*) that he _____ (*might meet*) a real star soon.
4 Olivia told us we _____ (*must take*) a lot of pictures if we got close to a celebrity.
5 Peter said that celebrities _____ (*shouldn't charge*) money for pictures or autographs.
6 Ana admitted that she _____ (*will probably never be*) famous.

B Look at the status update. Complete the message.

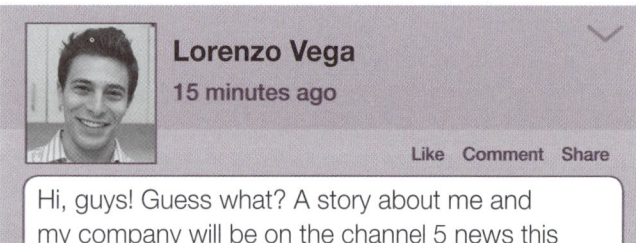

Lorenzo Vega
15 minutes ago

Like   Comment   Share

Hi, guys! Guess what? A story about me and my company will be on the channel 5 news this afternoon! It might help our business a lot, or at least it can't hurt. Anyway, I had planned to watch it at work, and I still would watch it if I could, but there's an important meeting I absolutely must attend. Can someone please record it for me? Thanks! The story should be on about 4:45 today.

Hi, Mom! Do you remember my friend Lorenzo? Well, he just told me that he (1) _____ be on the channel 5 news today! He said the story (2) _____ help his company a lot, or at least it (3) _____ hurt. Lorenzo explained that he (4) _____ to watch the story at work, and he said he still (5) _____ watch it if he (6) _____, but there's a problem. He told me he (7) _____ attend an important meeting. He asked if someone (8) _____ record the story for him. I'm at work, so I can't do it. Can you help, Mom? Lorenzo said the story (9) _____ be on at 4:45 today. Thanks! Kylie

2 VOCABULARY: ways to become famous

A Choose the correct option to complete the ways to become famous.

1 She inherited a *cure* / *fortune* worth millions.
2 She broke a world *record* / *scandal* in women's soccer.
3 He caused a *novel* / *scandal* that embarrassed his entire family.
4 She came up with a new *invention* / *novel* that helps people save energy.
5 He's a business leader who runs a global *company* / *record*.
6 He discovered *a cure* / *an invention* for a disease.
7 She wrote a best-selling *novel* / *record* about her experiences in Africa.

B Match the sentences (1–7) in Exercise A with the sentences (a–g) below. Write the correct number of the sentence from Exercise A.

a) ___ He found a plant that might stop cancer.
b) ___ She made a car that doesn't need gas.
c) ___ She's scored more goals than anyone else in history.
d) ___ Millions of people bought her book.
e) ___ He runs an airline that flies to 51 countries.
f) ___ He cheated on a popular quiz show.
g) ___ Her uncle died and left her his business.

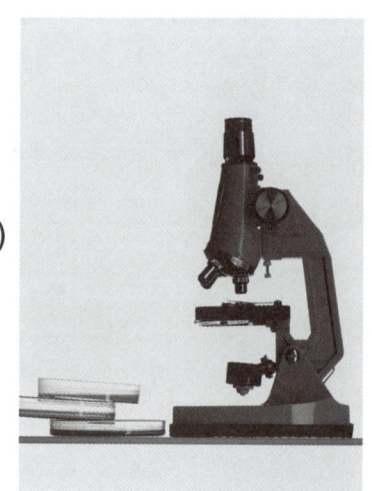

3 READING: for different purposes

A Match the ways of reading with the definitions.

1 skimming
2 scanning
3 reading in detail

a) reading a text carefully to learn concepts and details
b) looking quickly at a text to get a general idea of what it's about
c) looking for specific information in a text

B Read the questions and answer them using an appropriate method from Exercise A. Write a, b, or c to indicate which method you chose.

1 ___ What type of famous person is the article about? _____
2 ___ What have some of them helped to sell? _____
3 ___ Who thinks the original advertisement was a bad idea? _____
4 ___ When did Jenn Morris experience a big success? _____
5 ___ How many times has Luc Longley been in the Olympics? _____

Sporting Week

Home   **News**   **Science**   **Technology**   **Environment**   **Politics**   **Sports**

Athletes Fight Back Over McDonald's Olympic Games Ads

A *controversy* has broken out after a number of top Australian athletes, including Australian race walker Nathan Deakes, appeared in advertisements for McDonald's hamburgers during the *run-up* to the Olympic Games. In his ad, Deakes said that just after competing in the Olympic Games, he'd eaten a McDonald's hamburger as his post-race meal. He said it reminded him of his childhood, when his parents had taken him to McDonald's after practice. He also said that he'd really *looked forward* to having a McDonald's *milkshake* after competing. The ads are part of McDonald's advertising campaign during the current Olympics, which includes a special Olympic burger, as well as a "Champion Kids" *promotion*.

[2]However, in response to these ads, two leading Australian newspapers have run *one-time* counter ads featuring the famous basketball player and former Olympic athlete Luc Longley and the Olympic hockey gold medalist Jenn Morris. In the ad featuring Morris, she said that it was hard to describe how she had felt after scoring the final goal in the final game in Sydney, but that the last thing she had thought about was milkshakes, fries, and burgers. She went on to say that when she was young, after-practice food meant oranges, not junk food.

[3]Morris, who works for Western Australia's Healthway health promotion organization, said it was very disappointing to see the way that sports champions were being used to sell this type of food.

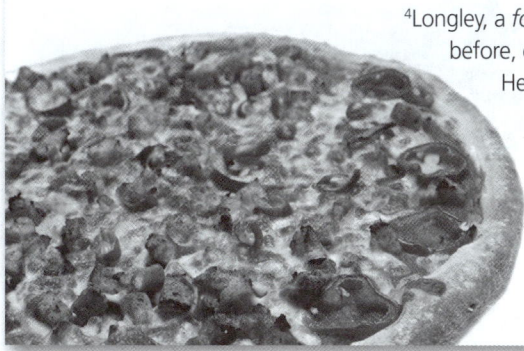

[4]Longley, a *former* three-time Olympian, said the idea of eating fast food before, or after, an Olympic competition had never entered his mind. He pointed out that jumping to reach the basketball *hoop* was hard enough without a stomach full of heavy food.

[5]The anti-junk food advertisements were funded by a number of prominent Australian health organizations.

Adapted from www.crikey.com.au

4 VOCABULARY: guessing meaning from context

Read the sentences and choose the correct meaning of the words in bold.

1 My savings have been **dwindling** over the last few months, a few dollars a day.
   a) decreasing slowly   b) decreasing rapidly

2 Many celebrities find being famous so **traumatic** that they need psychological help.
   a) having an extremely negative effect   b) having a slightly negative effect

3 It's troubling that more and more young children have **aspirations** to be famous when they are adults.
   a) something you want to achieve in the future   b) something you want to do right now

4 Many celebrities who **make it big** find that having lots of money and fans still doesn't make them happy.
   a) become rich, but not famous   b) become rich and famous

5 Being **in the spotlight** has good and bad points; one day the media praises you, and they next day they criticize you.
   a) well-known and well-loved   b) well-known, but not always well-loved

6 After three decades of fame and attention, the actor suddenly found himself **washed-up** and forgotten.
   a) no longer famous   b) famous as a child, but not as an adult

7 Many stars are depressed when they aren't on stage and feel a deep sense of **worthlessness**.
   a) a sad feeling   b) an angry feeling

8 Unfortunately, many celebrities don't realize that true **self-esteem** comes from within, not from others.
   a) loving yourself   b) being loved by others

5 GRAMMAR: reported speech — optional back-shifting

A Look at the sentences. For each sentence, is back-shifting O (optional) or N (necessary)? Write the correct letter.

1 ___ "Reality TV and celebrity gossip magazines are more popular than ever."
2 ___ "We'll all be famous pop stars in five years."
3 ___ "Those two actresses are wearing the same dress."
4 ___ "Jay-Z is never going to be a successful rapper."
5 ___ "It takes talent, hard work, and luck to succeed as an actor."

B Match the sentences in Exercise A with the reasons why back-shifting is optional or necessary. Write the number of the sentence in Exercise A.

a) The sentence reports a general truth. Back-shifting is optional. ___ ___
b) The sentence reports something that is true right now. Back-shifting is optional. ___
c) The sentence reports future possibilities or plans. Back-shifting is optional. ___
d) The sentence reports something that is no longer true. Back-shifting is necessary. ___

C Rewrite the sentence in Exercise A that needs back-shifting.

She said that _____.

WATCH OUT!

(X) They said she will never be famous, but years later she became a big star.

(✓) _____
_____
_____
_____

D Read the interview. Then choose the correct option to complete the report of the interview. If both choices are possible, choose both.

Man: Olivia Smart, welcome. Do you think you'll win tonight?

Olivia: I don't know. I'm probably not going to win, but I really want this award. I'm wearing my lucky earrings!

Man: Why is this award so special to you?

Olivia: Well, every actress dreams of winning this award. You know, this business isn't easy. I remember my family told me, "You'll never be a star in Hollywood." But they were wrong!

Man: What will you do if you win?

Olivia: I'll probably cry a lot!

"I've just spoken to Olivia Smart. She said **(1)** *she's probably not going to win / she probably wasn't going to win*, but she also admitted that she really **(2)** *wants / wanted* this award. And she said **(3)** *she's wearing / she was wearing* her lucky earrings, so maybe that will help! She also told us that every actress **(4)** *dreams / dreamed* of winning this award and added that the entertainment business **(5)** *isn't / wasn't* easy. Her family told her that she **(6)** *will never be / would never be* a star in Hollywood, but they were wrong. Finally, Olivia predicted that she **(7)** *will cry / would cry* a lot if she wins the award tonight. So, will Olivia Smart be crying for joy later tonight? I guess we'll just have to wait and see."

6 COMMUNICATION STRATEGY: clarifying misunderstandings

A Put the words in the correct order to make clarifications.

1 meant / actually, / I / that's / what / not

_____

2 easy / fame / way / isn't / put / that / it

_____

3 I'm / maybe / myself / not / making / clear

_____

4 that / I / perhaps / rephrase / should

_____

5 complicated / what / I / was / meant / it's

_____

6 it's / a problem / is / say / to / I'm / what / trying

_____

B 🎧 08 Listen and guess what the final part of each conversation will be.

1 ___   2 ___   3 ___   4 ___   5 ___   6 ___

a) Well, perhaps I should rephrase that—he's one of the greatest athletes ever.

b) What I'm trying to say is, fame makes it hard for famous people to maintain relationships with non-celebrities because their lives are so different.

c) Actually, that's not what I meant. She's got some talent. She's good at promoting herself. But he's just so much more talented.

d) Talent used to come first, put it that way. In the past, kids wanted to be famous for being good at something. Now they just want fame!

e) Maybe I'm not making myself clear. I don't read horror books at all. They're too scary for me!

f) Well, what I meant was, you can come up with your own idea, like sitting in a tree for the longest time or something, and then do it, and you get famous!

C 🎧 09 Listen to the complete conversations and check your answers.

skillsStudio

A Read the article about three famous Englishmen and answer the questions.

1 Check the people in the article who were definitely real.
☐ Sherlock Holmes
☐ Winston Churchill
☐ King Arthur

2 Who did most of the young people in the survey *think* were real? Check the names.
☐ Sherlock Holmes
☐ Winston Churchill
☐ King Arthur

B Read the text again. Find a synonym for each of these words in the paragraphs indicated.

1 lack of understanding (paragraph A):
_____

2 not real (paragraph B):
_____

3 valuable object (paragraph C):
_____

4 encouraged (paragraph D):
_____

C Read the text again and choose the correct sentence for each blank. There is one extra sentence that you do not need to use.

a) However, some scholars say there is evidence that he really existed.
b) We shall never surrender.
c) Researchers asked 3,000 people under 20 about real, historical figures and also characters from stories.
d) The books are still popular today, and some of the most famous have been made into movies and TV shows.
e) You might name John Lennon or Paul McCartney of the Beatles, or perhaps a famous athlete like David Beckham.

D Match (1–6) with options from (a–i) to make complete sentences. There are three extra options that you do not need to use.

1 Researchers asked 3,000 young people about

2 Sir Arthur Conan Doyle was

3 People around the world

4 The Knights of the Round Table were

5 Churchill gave his most famous speeches

6 Twenty percent of British teenagers

a) send letters to Sherlock Holmes.
b) believe that Churchill wasn't real.
c) told researchers that Holmes was real.
d) in the late 1800s and early 1900s.
e) in the early 1940s.
f) real and fictional Englishmen.
g) King Arthur's trusted followers.
h) the author of the Sherlock Holmes stories.
i) Sherlock Holmes' assistant.

E Write an opinion essay of about 250 words on the following statement:

"It isn't important for people to know whether characters are real or not.
Fictional characters can provide true inspiration, and that's all that matters."

World-famous Englishmen:
Real or fictional?

If you were asked to name three famous English people, who would be on your list? (1) _____ **You might name Sherlock Holmes, Sir Winston Churchill, or even King Arthur.**

A Researchers who wanted to learn more about what the U.K.'s young people know about their own famous countrymen and women have made an interesting discovery. After surveying 3,000 British people under the age of 20, researchers learned that, although young people do know the names and adventures of Holmes, Churchill, and Arthur, there is confusion about which of the men are real and which are fictional characters.

B *Sherlock Holmes*

One of the most famous Englishmen in the world is Sherlock Holmes, a 19th-Century detective who, in fact, never really existed. Created by author Sir Arthur Conan Doyle, Holmes and his assistant, Dr. Watson, were fictional characters who lived in London in the late 1800s and early 1900s. Holmes began working as a detective in 1887, and his fame grew quickly due to his ability to solve difficult crimes through careful observation and the use of logic. Watson wrote books telling the stories of some of the cases Holmes solved. **(2)** _____ There is even a Sherlock Holmes museum at 221b Baker Street, London, an address made famous as the house where Holmes lived and worked.

Given the detective's great fame, and the fact that his fictional house can be found at a real address in London, perhaps it's not surprising that researchers found that 58 percent of British teenagers believed Holmes was a real person. These young British people are not alone in their confusion, either. Through the years, people around the world have sent letters to Sherlock Holmes at 221b Baker Street, asking for his help.

C *King Arthur*

Another famous Englishman that the researchers asked about was King Arthur. Legends tell of the huge, round table where the great king sat with his most trusted knights—known, perhaps not surprisingly, as the Knights of the Round Table. But why a round table? Because at a round table, no one has the most important seat, and everyone is equal. Arthur's best-known adventure might be his search for the Holy Grail, a holy treasure. They searched for years, but unfortunately their quest ended in defeat.

According to the stories, Arthur lived in the 5th or 6th Century. But was he real? In the same survey of British teenagers, 65% said he was real. The experts aren't sure, however. Many historians believe Arthur was invented by a writer in the 12th Century. **(3)** _____

D *Sir Winston Churchill*

Researchers also asked the subjects of their survey about the British leader Winston Churchill. Churchill, born in 1874, worked in the government most of his adult life, but he is best remembered for his courage and leadership of Great Britain in the dark years of 1940–1945, during World War II. The speeches that he gave as Prime Minister inspired the British people, and he will always be remembered as one of the country's toughest fighters and greatest leaders. "We shall go on to the end," he declared in 1940 in one of his most famous speeches. "We shall fight on the seas and oceans, … we shall fight on the beaches, … we shall fight in the fields and in the streets, … **(4)** _____."

There are pictures, recordings, and film of Churchill's speeches and yet, in the survey of British teenagers, 20% said he was a fictional character.

UNIT 4   UPS AND DOWNS

1 LISTENING: understanding discourse markers

A 🎧 **10** **Listen to the podcast and choose T (true) or F (false).**

1   The happiest country in the world according to the OECD is Norway.   T / F
2   The OECD surveys people in 11 different countries.   T / F
3   Six hundred thousand people have answered the survey.   T / F
4   The most important thing to most people is life satisfaction.   T / F
5   Greece ranks 34th in the list of countries.   T / F
6   Life in Turkey has improved recently for its citizens.   T / F

B **Listen again. Number the discourse markers (a–l) in the order that you hear them.**

a) In addition   ☐   g) Furthermore   ☐
b) As a result   ☐   h) As a consequence   ☐
c) In general   ☐   i) To a great extent   ☐
d) On the other hand   ☐   j) Consequently   ☐
e) On the whole   ☐   k) Nevertheless   ☐
f) That said   ☐   l) What's more   ☐

C **Write the letters of the discourse markers from Exercise B next to their correct function.**

1   To talk generally: ___, ___, ___
2   To introduce a contrasting point: ___, ___, ___
3   To introduce a result: ___, ___, ___
4   To introduce an additional point: ___, ___, ___

2 VOCABULARY: life satisfaction

A **Write the words from the box in the correct blanks below.**

> appreciate   appreciation   content   contentment   enjoy   enjoyment
> happiness   happy   pleasant   pleasure   satisfaction   satisfy   wealth   wealthy

Nouns: _____, _____, _____, _____, _____,
              _____, _____

Adjectives: _____, _____, _____, _____

Verbs: _____, _____, _____

B Complete the sentences with one of the words from Exercise A. For some sentences more than one answer is possible.

1 Did you _____ your trip to Spain?
2 He used to be a _____ man, but he lost his fortune in the stock market crash.
3 It was with great _____ that the teacher gave her students their scores.
4 Joe is very _____ when he's away from the city.
5 We really _____ the effort that you've made for us.
6 Some people think the most important thing in life is money, but for me it's _____.
7 We were having a very _____ day until we got lost.

3 GRAMMAR: noun clauses as objects

A Replace the words in parentheses with one of the words from the box.

how what when where why

1 Can you tell me (*the time that*) _____ the movie starts?
2 I don't know (*the reason that*) _____ he's in such a good mood today.
3 Do you know (*the way that*) _____ he became so wealthy?
4 Tell me (*the place that*) _____ you want to meet.
5 I appreciate (*the things that*) _____ you've done for me.

B Choose the correct option to complete the sentences.

1 I don't understand _____ I'm feeling so happy, but I'm not complaining!
   a) what   b) why   c) when
2 I feel very angry about _____ I was treated during my trip.
   a) when   b) where   c) how
3 Could you let me know _____ the best time to call would be?
   a) when   b) how   c) why
4 The students couldn't hear _____ the lecturer was saying.
   a) why   b) when   c) what
5 Do you remember _____ you were when you last saw your keys?
   a) what   b) where   c) why

WATCH OUT!

✗ I don't know where did he go.

✓ I don't know _____

C Complete the phone conversation with words from Exercise A.

Ann: Hi! Do you want to come to a life skills seminar with me tonight?

José: Sure! Do you know **(1)** _____ it's about?

Ann: Well, the title is, "Understanding yourself and your emotions." So, I guess it's about **(2)** _____ we feel the way we do.

José: Cool. Did you check **(3)** _____ it starts? I hope it's not too late!

Ann: It isn't. It's at 7:15. I don't know **(4)** _____ it's being held, but Dave said it would probably be in the Arts Center. I'll check, OK?

José: Great. Do you know **(5)** _____ you're getting there? Do you want to meet first and go together?

Ann: Sounds good!

4 VOCABULARY: mood

A))🎧11 **Listen and write the words and phrases you hear.**

1 _____   5 _____
2 _____   6 _____
3 _____   7 _____
4 _____   8 _____

B **Complete the sentences with words or phrases from Exercise A.**

1 I just can't concentrate on my work today—I don't know why I'm so _____, but I need to be more _____ so that I can finish this essay.

2 Sam always sees the best in every situation because she's so _____. Her husband, Costas, is much more negative and always expects the worst—he's very _____.

3 Kao's _____ have been very up and down since he moved to the city, but he's trying to achieve a _____ so that he can look to the future and move on with his life.

4 Whenever I'm feeling low and _____, I talk to Jon because he's always _____ and he always cheers me up.

5 GRAMMAR: review of conditional forms

A **Complete the grammar rules.**

> **Zero conditional**: to talk about things that are generally true
> If + **(1)** _____, simple present
> **1st conditional**: to talk about things that are likely or possible in the future
> If + **(2)** _____, will (won't) + base form
> **2nd conditional**: to talk about things that are unreal or unlikely in the present or future
> If + **(3)** _____, + would(n't) + base form
> **3rd conditional**: to talk about unreal situations in the past
> If + **(4)** _____, would(n't) have + past participle

B **Complete the sentences with the correct forms of the verbs in parentheses.**

1 I've never seen the movie. I _____ (cry) if I _____ (watch) it last night.

2 Denise might see Karl today. If she _____ (see) him, she _____ (tell) him your good news.

3 I'm unhappy because I don't have enough money. If I _____ (be) wealthy, I _____ (be) very happy.

4 I saw Chi today, but I didn't know he was depressed. If he _____ (tell) me, I _____ (could/help) him.

5 If you _____ (have) good friends, they always _____ (help) if you have problems.

6 If you _____ (not/take) this opportunity, you _____ (regret) it.

> **WATCH OUT!**
>
> ⊗ If you tell me he was depressed, I would have called him.
>
> ⊘ _____
> _____
> _____

C This conversation contains six mistakes with conditional forms. Find the mistakes and correct them.

Chris: What are you reading?

Lisa: It's an article called *The Key to Happiness*. I read you some sections if you're interested.

Chris: All right.

Lisa: OK, well, it says that if you wanted to be happy, then be a good friend, because strong relationships are the key to contentment.

Chris: I think that's true. I love spending time with my friends and if I didn't have them, I will be very unhappy.

Lisa: Me, too. It also says that people are usually more satisfied with life if they did a job that they love.

Chris: Yeah, that's true, too. Do you remember last year when I was doing that office job I hated? If I hadn't gotten a new job in the music store, I will still be miserable.

Lisa: Hmm, and probably the reason I'm not that happy right now is because I don't have a job I enjoy. I think if I have a job that I love, then I would be more content.

Chris: I totally agree. So, stop reading that article, and check out the job postings instead!

Lisa: Good point!

6 WRITING: a thank-you note

A Put the words in the correct order to make expressions used in thank-you notes.

1 generous / your / so / was / donation

   _____

2 express / I / for / gratitude / also / my / would / to / like

   _____

3 again / of / thanks / all / us / here / from

   _____

4 you / writing / I / to / for / am / thank

   _____

B Read Cecilia's thank-you note. Complete each blank with an expression from Exercise A.

To: Simon Barbier   **From:** Cecilia Harris
Re: Crowdfunding donation

Dear Mr. Barbier,
(1) _____ your contribution to our Crowdfunding Project to raise money to set up a new community center for unemployed young people. It's great that local business leaders are taking an interest in the project.
(2) _____ and has helped us on our way to achieving our final target. We are hoping to open the center next summer, and we'll keep you updated on our progress.
(3) _____ your kind offer to deliver a talk at the center once it is up and running. I think this would be very beneficial, and that our members would learn a great deal from hearing about your business experiences. I'll be in touch to arrange details at a later date.
(4) _____
Sincerely,
Cecilia Harris

skillsStudio

A Read the opinions and decide whether the speakers are optimistic or pessimistic.

> 1 "I'm in my early 20s and I find it difficult to get excited about the future. There's so much unemployment in my country and I don't know if there'll be a job for me when I finish school. I find the uncertainty very hard to live with."

☐ optimistic   ☐ pessimistic

> 2 "Well, I'm in my mid 40s now and I've never felt better. I've gotten over the insecurities of my early 20s, so I can really enjoy life to the fullest now."

☐ optimistic   ☐ pessimistic

> 3 "I was really happy when I was in my early 20s. Then life got me down a little bit as I went through middle age, but I've come out on the other side, and now I'm in my late 60s. I'm happier than I've ever been. My body may not be as young as it used to be, but the future looks bright!"

☐ optimistic   ☐ pessimistic

B 🎧 **12** Susie is discussing a report with her grandfather, Ron, about satisfaction levels at different stages of life. Listen once and answer these questions.

1 According to the report, what are the two ages that we feel happiest in life?

_____ , _____

2 Which speaker from Exercise A agrees with the findings of the report?

_____

C Listen again and match the words and phrases you heard in the conversation (1–6) with their definitions (a–f).

1	peak	a)	think something is worse or less important than it really is
2	make the most of	b)	reach its highest or greatest level
3	overestimate	c)	follow
4	underestimate	d)	think something is better or more important than it really is
5	pursue	e)	enjoy or use something as much as possible
6	generalize	f)	say something about a group of people or things that is true for most of them

D Listen again and choose the correct options to complete the table.

Age	According to report, our satisfaction levels are …	Ron's opinion of report findings
23	**(1)** *high / low / increasing / declining.*	**(2)** He *agrees / disagrees / doesn't say.*
30s and 40s	**(3)** *high / low / increasing / declining.*	**(4)** He *agrees / disagrees / doesn't say.*
Mid 50s	**(5)** *high / low / increasing / declining.*	**(6)** He *agrees / disagrees / doesn't say.*
After 55	**(7)** *high / low / increasing / declining.*	**(8)** He *agrees / disagrees / doesn't say.*
69	**(9)** *high / low / increasing / declining.*	**(10)** He *agrees / disagrees / doesn't say.*
After 75	**(11)** *high / low / increasing / declining.*	**(12)** He *agrees / disagrees / doesn't say.*

E Listen again and choose the correct answer.

1 According to the report, 23-year-olds predict that they will be … in the future than they really will be.
- **a)** 10% more satisfied
- **b)** 10% less satisfied
- **c)** 10% more disappointed
- **d)** 10% less disappointed

2 According to the report, people in their mid 50s feel sad because they realize that …
- **a)** they won't be able to make the dreams of their youth a reality.
- **b)** they are getting older.
- **c)** their bodies are not able to do what they used to do.
- **d)** they need to have lower expectations in life.

3 When Ron was 53, he …
- **a)** got a new job in sales.
- **b)** became a yoga instructor.
- **c)** realized his dreams weren't going to come true.
- **d)** had a career change that made him more wealthy.

4 According to the report, people who are 69 …
- **a)** are less happy than they were when they were younger because they expect more from life.
- **b)** are happier than they were when they were younger because they expect less from life.
- **c)** are happier than they were when they were younger because they are so wise.
- **d)** are happier than they were when they were younger because they do yoga.

5 The report was based on data from … people.
- **a)** 21,161
- **b)** 23,151
- **c)** 23,161
- **d)** 20,161

6 They spoke to people from east and west Germany, and the results were … the people were from different backgrounds.
- **a)** exactly the same even though
- **b)** completely different even though
- **c)** completely different because
- **d)** almost the same even though

F Do you agree or disagree with the findings of the report that Susie talked about? Write an online comment of about 200 words in response to the article.

UNIT 5 SOMETHING IN THE WATER

1 GRAMMAR: the passive

A Match each tense (1–5) with the correct form of the passive (a–e).

1 simple present
2 simple past
3 present progressive
4 present perfect
5 past perfect

a) Beijing's Olympic pool is still being used, years after the Games.
b) It is located near the Bird's Nest Stadium.
c) The pool has been transformed into a water park.
d) The Olympic Games were held there in 2008.
e) The original pool hadn't been designed as a water park.

B Choose the correct options to complete the article.

Beijing's Water Cube Transformed

When the Beijing Olympic pool **(1)** *has been built / was first built*, it was called The Water Cube due to its extraordinary cube-shaped exterior. Now, several years after the Olympics, the inside is just as incredible. The place where Michael Phelps **(2)** *has been awarded / was awarded* eight gold medals **(3)** *has been transformed / is transformed* into an enormous indoor water park—the largest in Asia. It already has waterslides, a wave pool, and an indoor river, and new rides **(4)** *were added / are being added* every year. The site, which **(5)** *is now called / is now being called* Happy Magic Water Park, **(6)** *was designed / is being designed* to look like an underwater environment and is decorated with colorful jellyfish, coral, and floating bubbles. Unlike sites in other Olympic cities, the Water Cube **(7)** *hasn't been abandoned / hadn't been abandoned* for long before it **(8)** *was redesigned / had been redesigned*, so the transformation was not difficult. Since it opened, the park **(9)** *was visited / has been visited* by more than two million people, and it is the second most popular tourist spot in China, after the Great Wall. Beijing residents say they are glad this wonderful building **(10)** *has still been used / is still being used* and enjoyed by so many people.

WATCH OUT!

 Dozens of homes were damaging by the flood.

✓ _____

C Complete the email with the correct form of the passive. Use the verbs and words in parentheses.

To: Igor   **From:** Aliyu
Subject: Hi from Jordan!

Hi, Igor! Greetings from the hot springs in Jordan! This place is so cool. It **(1)** _____ (*locate*) in an oasis near the Dead Sea. Even though we're in the middle of the desert, there is a lot of water here. The water comes from a small desert river, as well as from several hot spring waterfalls. The spa **(2)** _____ (*build*) a few years ago because people say the warm, salty water is good for your health. This afternoon, I **(3)** _____ (*give*) a two-hour Six Senses massage with warm water and mud from the sea. So therapeutic!

The spa is beautiful, and they're making changes to it all the time. Right now, the walls inside the hotel **(4)** _____ (*paint*) in natural colors, and my room **(5)** _____ (*recently/ decorate*). It's like an Arabian palace! Yesterday morning, I lay by the pool in the canyon. Then I had an incredible lunch on the terrace, overlooking the waterfalls. An organic vegetable garden **(6)** _____ (*just/plant*) on the grounds, so fresh vegetables **(7)** _____ (*always/serve*) in the restaurants. Unfortunately, I fell asleep after that and missed dinner. It was supposed to be a special "Bedouin-style" meal by candlelight in the olive grove, but when I got there all the food **(8)** _____ (*clear away*)! I'll upload some pictures for you to look at soon. Take care, Aliyu

2 READING: inferring opinion

A Read about three hotels. Write the paragraph heading next to the name of the hotel.

a) Pamper yourself in a glamorous getaway

b) Spend the night in a hotel made of frozen water

c) Head underwater for a unique experience

The best hotels *on (and under!) the water*

Everyone loves to take a vacation by the sea, but for some travelers, even a five-star beach resort isn't enough. If you're one of those tourists, you might give these hotels a try.

1 Jules' Underwater Lodge: _____

Originally a research lab, the lodge is set entirely under water at the bottom of a lagoon in Florida. Guests wishing to stay there have to scuba dive 21 feet below the surface of the water—those not able to scuba dive are required to take a short course first. The lodge has the kind of comforts you'd expect to see in any hotel, such as hot showers, phones, TVs, and a well-stocked kitchen. But what **(1)** <u>sets it apart</u> is the view of the rich and varied marine life swimming past the windows. **(2)** <u>For the lucky few who get to stay there</u>, it's this view that has the most profound effect. Many describe the experience as the most incredible of their lives.

2 The Burj Al-Arab Hotel: _____

In the pristine waters of the Arabian Gulf stands the Burj Al-Arab, the world's first seven-star hotel. Opened for the millennium, it has been designed like a ship's sail. Here you can find 202 luxurious suites, infinity pools, chauffeured shopping, personal butlers, helicopter tours … **(3)** <u>And that's just the beginning</u> … Don't forget to visit the underwater restaurant—accessed by a submarine—and enjoy your dinner in the company of sharks. If **(4)** <u>that's not up your alley</u>, be sure to visit the Burj Al-Arab's upstairs restaurant one evening, if only to admire the view. Gaze over the Persian Gulf and the extraordinary man-made Palm Islands below.

3 Hotel de Glace: _____

If you want to stay on the water, this hotel near Quebec City in Canada offers **(5)** <u>a unique twist</u>: the entire hotel is made of ice. Hotel de Glace is French for "Ice Hotel," and it is open only during the winter months. The cafe, bar, and restaurant are all made of ice, as are the tables, chairs, and beds. The rooms have beautiful ice sculptures and, for those **(6)** <u>who have had their fill of</u> frozen things, fireplaces. For obvious reasons, the fireplaces are not made of ice.

B Read the texts in Exercise A again. Choose the best definition for the underlined phrases.

1 a) makes it special	**b)** puts it a long distance away
2 a) a few people who stay there have good fortune	**b)** not many people have the opportunity to stay there
3 a) the end of your stay is different	**b)** the hotel offers much more than this
4 a) you are staying in a different place	**b)** you don't like that kind of thing
5 a) an interesting variation	**b)** a hotel that rotates
6 a) who do not want any more	**b)** who really enjoy

3 VOCABULARY: marketing

A 🎧 **13** **Listen to the conversation in a restaurant. Why doesn't the man want to order bottled water?**

a) It costs too much.　　**b)** It's bad for the environment.　　**c)** both of these reasons

B **Listen again. Put the phrases related to marketing in the order that you hear them (1–5).**

☐ range from … to …
☐ market … as …
☐ make … worth …
☐ put up against …
☐ as much about … as …

C **Complete the contribution to the online debate using the words from Exercise B.**

LOGIN

| HOME | FORUMS | PROFILE | ABOUT |

enviroKING
Join date: Nov 2003
Location: San Diego
Posts: 2091

July 31 11:53 a.m.
Given the lack of water on this planet, I think the price of bottled water is not high enough! Where I live, the price of a bottle of water usually **(1)** _____ $1.00 _____ $2.50. That's nothing to people here. Even worse, companies **(2)** _____ bottled water _____ something you buy to use the contents and then throw away the packaging. So people waste water and pollute the environment with plastic trash. People need to think twice before buying bottled water. As consumers, our choices should be **(3)** _____ helping the planet _____ our own convenience.

Jenny497
Join date: Jan 2008
Location: London
Posts: 147

July 31 12:08 p.m.
I agree with you to a certain extent. We should conserve water and reduce trash. But is bottled water too cheap? No way! Companies are selling it for $5, $6, even $10 a bottle now. When you **(4)** _____ bottled water _____ other products like cooking oil or even gasoline, it's actually extremely expensive. **(5)** _____ a simple bottle of water _____ that kind of money, the bottle would have to be made of gold! People should just buy a reusable bottle and refill it with water from home.

4 COMMUNICATION STRATEGY: suggesting alternatives

A **Choose the correct expressions to complete the text.**

Kirsten: Look at this. What can we do to raise awareness about water pollution?

Tim: We could try **(1)** *collecting / collect* some trash from the river and displaying it.

Kirsten: I like that idea! I'd suggest **(2)** *to put / putting* it on display by the river.

Tim: Maybe, but the trash might fall into the river again. What about **(3)** *display / displaying* it somewhere indoors? There **(4)** *is / was* always the school.

Jess: No, not the school. Since adult shoppers throw most of the trash in the river, let's focus on them. Have you considered **(5)** *give / giving* the shopping mall a try?

Tim: Nice idea, but I don't think the mall would accept the trash. Hey, what if we **(6)** *take / taking* pictures of the trash instead? We could display pictures in the mall.

Jess: Or another option would be to **(7)** *hand / handing* out leaflets …

B 🎧 **14** **Listen to the conversation and check your answers.**

Stop water pollution!

Help us raise awareness.

5 GRAMMAR: expressions of purpose

A Complete the structures with the words and phrases from the box.

> base form   gerund   noun + clause

1 *for +* _____
2 *in order (not) to +* _____
3 *so as (not) to +* _____
4 *so (that) +* _____
5 *to +* _____

B Complete the facts about water using the structures in Exercise A. More than one answer is possible in some cases.

Water facts

Water is important **(1)** _____ transporting nutrients around your body. It is also needed for good digestion, circulation, and temperature control among other functions. Lack of water can cause headaches, poor concentration, and many other issues. That's why it's important to drink enough water and stay hydrated. Experts say that you need to drink about eight cups of water every day. Here are a few tips for getting enough water every day:

Eating fruit is ideal **(2)** _____ help you receive your eight cups, and soup is also great **(3)** _____ including more liquids in your diet.

(4) _____ be healthy, avoid drinking too much caffeine. Drink plain water or herbal infusions. When you feel thirsty, your body has already lost 1% of its total water. Drink water throughout exercise **(5)** _____ you don't dehydrate.

Be careful in hot weather. **(6)** _____ become dehydrated, drink water every hour—even if you don't feel thirsty.

6 VOCABULARY: environmental issues

A Put the letters into the correct order to make words and phrases.

1 rawet nulloptio _____
2 namefi _____
3 neeghiy _____
4 odflo _____
5 trawe trovepy _____
6 grudtho _____
7 essadie _____
8 limecat enchag _____

B Complete the text using the correct form of the words from Exercise A.

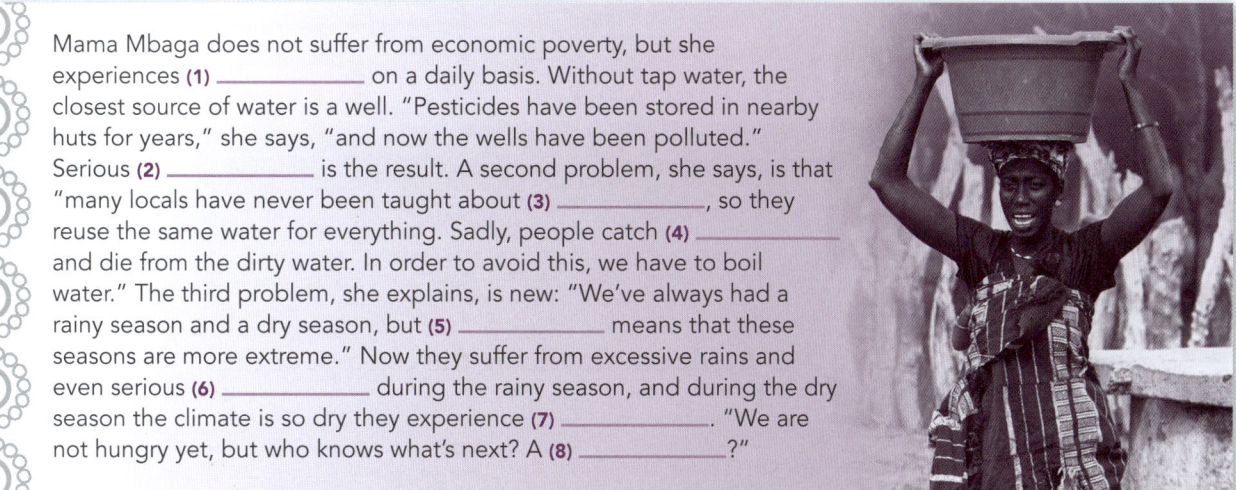

Mama Mbaga does not suffer from economic poverty, but she experiences **(1)** _____ on a daily basis. Without tap water, the closest source of water is a well. "Pesticides have been stored in nearby huts for years," she says, "and now the wells have been polluted." Serious **(2)** _____ is the result. A second problem, she says, is that "many locals have never been taught about **(3)** _____, so they reuse the same water for everything. Sadly, people catch **(4)** _____ and die from the dirty water. In order to avoid this, we have to boil water." The third problem, she explains, is new: "We've always had a rainy season and a dry season, but **(5)** _____ means that these seasons are more extreme." Now they suffer from excessive rains and even serious **(6)** _____ during the rainy season, and during the dry season the climate is so dry they experience **(7)** _____. "We are not hungry yet, but who knows what's next? A **(8)** _____?"

skillsStudio

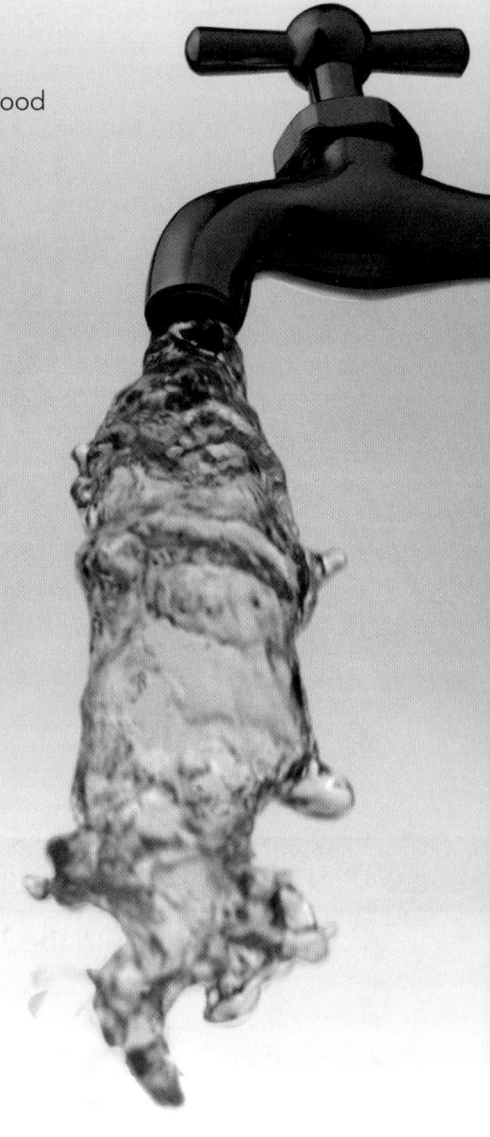

A Read the article and choose the best title.

1 Check out your water footprint!
2 Water footprinting—a new approach to water conservation
3 Global water poverty continues to grow

B Choose the correct definition of a water footprint.

1 A measurement of water volume consumed and/or polluted per item of food
2 The total volume of fresh water used to produce goods and services
3 A geographical indicator to indicate where water was used to produce items

C Read the article again. Underline the sentence that expresses the main idea in each paragraph.

D Read the text again and answer these questions.

1 The phrase *as a consequence* in lines 1–2 means …
  a) however.
  b) similarly.
  c) because of this.
  d) in spite of.

2 In the second paragraph, the author suggests that people don't realize that …
  a) global warming also causes water poverty.
  b) the issue of water resources is as important as global warming.
  c) manufacturers are wasting water in order to reduce their carbon footprints.
  d) the World Bank is more concerned with water poverty than global warming.

3 Which of the following is an example of the indirect use of water?
  a) eating fruit
  b) washing your car
  c) using less hot water in the shower
  d) drinking water

4 If something is *scarce* (line 29), this means …
  a) it is not used efficiently.
  b) people only use it indirectly.
  c) there is not very much of it.
  d) it is bad for the environment.

5 The phrase *per capita* (line 34) probably means …
  a) for each person.
  b) annually.
  c) indirectly.
  d) inside its borders.

E Write a blog post of about 200 words summarizing the concept of the water footprint.

ENVIRONMENT

Issue 432

Over the last decade, international attention has been focused on global warming and climate change. As a consequence, most of us know the concept of the carbon footprint. In simple terms, the carbon footprint shows how much CO_2 is created by an individual, organization, or process. Today, many businesses and organizations calculate their carbon footprints and try to reduce the amount of CO_2 they produce.
5 Responsible consumers also calculate their personal carbon footprints. They then use this number to make better choices about the products they buy, the food they eat, and the way they travel.

There is, however, another global environmental issue that requires urgent international attention: water resources. Our planet has a limited amount of fresh water for drinking, hygiene, manufacturing, and farming. One of the main problems associated with this issue is water poverty: many people do not
10 have enough clean water for their basic needs. The World Bank has estimated that more than 700 million people in 43 countries are currently regularly affected by water poverty.

As a way of drawing society's attention to the nature and scale of the problem, scientists have developed the concept of the "water footprint." In the same way that a carbon footprint shows how much pollution an individual, organization, or process is responsible for, the water footprint shows how
15 much water an individual, organization, or process uses. The water footprint is calculated by adding two numbers: direct use and indirect use. The first part of the water footprint, direct use, is the water that we get directly from our faucets for drinking, cooking, and washing. Indirect use refers to the water used in the process of growing food and manufacturing the goods we buy such as paper, clothing, and so on. The water we use indirectly is known as "virtual water," and it is this water that is of increasing
20 concern. However, most people do not realize or think about the amount of water they use indirectly. For this reason, the idea of the water footprint is an important way to help people realize that their choices can have an impact on water poverty. It can also show people that small changes in lifestyle can make a difference.

Like carbon footprints, water footprints allow us to calculate our consumption, either as individuals or
25 as businesses. But water footprints have a wider variety of uses than carbon footprints. Water footprints can be calculated for specific goods and products. For example, we know that it takes 15,000 liters of water to produce a kilogram of beef and 2,400 for a hamburger. A cotton T-shirt requires 2,000 liters. In other words, when we import a T-shirt or eat a burger made from imported beef, we may be indirectly importing water from a region where water is already scarce. Water footprints can also help consumers
30 make choices that are better for the planet's water. For example, a vegetarian soy burger has a much smaller water footprint than the beef burger (160 liters, compared to 2,400).

Water footprints have also been calculated for each nation, with the result that we can compare international water consumption. The virtual water league table shows that the U.S. is the biggest offender, with a water footprint of almost 2,500 cubic meters per year per capita, while Britain's water
35 footprint is close to the global average of 1,243 cubic meters per year per capita. At 1,380 cubic meters per year per person, Japan's water footprint is relatively small; however, about 77% of that amount is from indirect use outside the country, meaning water consumed in producing the products imported by Japan. In comparison, about 20% of the United States' water footprint is used outside American borders. The creators of the water footprint hope that these numbers will create awareness and stimulate
40 international debate about ways that nations can use water more wisely.

Information source: www.waterfootprint.org

UNIT 6 LIVING TRADITIONS

1 GRAMMAR: *be used to / get used to*

A Choose the correct options to complete the sentences.

1 I've been living next door to the airport for three years, so I *'m used to /
'm getting used to* the noise now. I don't even notice it anymore.

2 I don't think I'll ever *be used to / get used to* commuting for three hours each day.
I don't like it and never will.

3 At first, the students didn't like the new tutor, but eventually they
were used to / got used to him.

4 When I first moved to the U.S., it took me a while to *be used to / get used to* driving,
but now it's fine.

5 Miranda was shocked because she *wasn't used to / didn't get used to* being
told what to do.

6 It took me a while, but I finally *was used to / got used to* the sound of the
waves.

B Complete the conversation with the correct form of *be used to*
or *get used to*.

Kay: Hi Jim. How are you settling in?

Jim: Pretty well, thanks. It's very different from my old job where there were
only eight of us in the company, but I **(1)** _____ being part of a
large organization slowly.

Kay: Hmm, whenever you start a new job, it always takes a while
(2) _____ a different working environment. And how are you
finding living in Japan? Moving here must have been a big culture
shock.

Jim: No, not at all. I did my training here, so I **(3)** _____ the local
customs and also I **(4)** _____ the language, because my wife
is Japanese.

Kay: That must make a big difference. I know that when I first arrived
here, it took me a while **(5)** _____ Japanese business
etiquette. It's very different from the way we do business in the U.S.

Jim: That's true, but no, I **(6)** _____ working with Japanese people,
so it's been easy for me to fit in.

WATCH OUT!

✗ I'm used to travel for my job.

✓ _____

2 LISTENING: for main ideas

A Read the description of the podcast and answer the questions.

searchallpodcasts

SEARCH

HOME

CATEGORIES

NEWEST

RECOMMENDED

MOST POPULAR

**Love and marriage in the 21st Century
(May 11, 8:00 p.m.)**

Is there still a place in today's society for weddings?
Are they an important tradition or an outdated
ritual? In this podcast, host Elsa Rains tries to gauge
public opinion by talking to people of various ages
and backgrounds. Her findings may surprise you.
Download, listen, and find out more.

25 mins [Download 15MB]

PLAY ▶   DOWNLOAD ⬇   PLAYLIST ♫   SHARE ⬀

1 The main purpose of this podcast is to …
   a) give advice to people who are
      getting married.
   b) question the role of weddings today.

2 On the podcast, we will probably hear …
   a) a lot of different people sharing their
      ideas.
   b) just the host Elsa Rains sharing
      her ideas.

3 We may hear vocabulary such as …
   a) wedding dress, tiara, wedding cake,
      first dance, and best man's toast.
   b) important, traditional, choice,
      thousands of dollars, and occasion.

B  🎧 **15** Listen to the interviews from the podcast.
Match each speaker with the main idea they express.

Speaker 1   **a)**   Weddings are an unnecessary expense for the couple and their guests.

Speaker 2   **b)**   Young people today have more important things to spend their money on.

Speaker 3   **c)**   Modern weddings are more flexible than traditional weddings.

Speaker 4   **d)**   Weddings are a necessary and exciting ritual.

3 VOCABULARY: institutional traditions

A 🎧 **16** Listen and write the words you hear.

1 _____   3 _____   5 _____

2 _____   4 _____   6 _____

B Write the words from Exercise A next to their synonyms.

1 ceremony, rite (*n.*): _____
2 introduction, induction (*n.*): _____
3 representative (*adj.*): _____
4 first-year student (*n.*): _____
5 good-luck symbol (*n.*): _____
6 upper-level (*adj.*): _____

C Complete the text with words from Exercise A in the correct form.

BLOG ON IT

SEARCH

FEATURES   BLOG   JOIN   LOGIN

HELEN SCHMIDT'S MILITARY ACADEMY BLOG

Saturday, August 28

My first week here has been pretty crazy. The older students have been playing tricks on the **(1)** _____. It's part of our **(2)** _____ into the school. Last night, they made us go out to a restaurant in our pajamas! It was a little embarrassing, but a lot of fun, too. Apparently this **(3)** _____ happens every year. The school's **(4)** _____ is a lion, so every morning, before we can have our breakfast, we have to practice making loud roaring noises. I'm getting pretty good at it! This is a picture of our principal. OK, everyone knows the principal has a **(5)** _____ job in the school, but because this is a military school, he also has a badge on his hat that is **(6)** _____ of his high position.

1 comment | add | related posts

4 GRAMMAR: verb + object + infinitive

A Put the words in the correct order to form sentences.

1 party / did / invite / he / to / you / his graduation / to / go

_____

2 for / late / to / morning / you / be / not / exercises / advise / I

_____

3 the students / be / ordered / the principal / quiet / to

_____

4 arrive / the ceremony / expect / to / they / the freshmen / on / for / time

_____

B Read the teacher's advice and complete the text below.

(1) I don't think you should worry too much about your exam next week.

(2) I think it would be a really good idea if you reviewed Chapter 8 of the textbook.

(3) Try to make sure that you get a good night's sleep the night before.

(4) I will let you use dictionaries during the exam.

(5) Remember that you must not bring cell phones into the exam room or you will fail.

(6) Come to my review class tomorrow! I think you'll find it very useful!

Professor Turner gave us some advice about preparing for the exam next week. He told **(1)** _____ too much about it. He advised **(2)** _____ Chapter 8 of the textbook and he encouraged **(3)** _____ a good night's sleep before the exam. He's going to allow **(4)** _____ dictionaries during the exam, but he warned **(5)** _____ cell phones into the exam room or we would fail. He invited **(6)** _____ to his review class the following day.

WATCH OUT!

Ⓧ They even ask us don't work too hard.

Ⓥ _____
_____
_____

5 VOCABULARY: phrasal verbs for personal rituals

A Match (1–8) with (a–h) to make complete sentences.

1 I cross things
2 I always line
3 Before we leave, we always plan
4 I always put
5 I always clean
6 I always write
7 Each morning, I go
8 I go

a) through my bag each night to check I haven't lost anything.
b) down everything I have to do each day.
c) on my lucky gloves before I play soccer.
d) up my mugs with the handles facing the same way.
e) off my list as I finish each job.
f) out what we're going to do on vacation.
g) out my athletic bag before every game.
h) over things I have to do that day.

B Complete the text with the correct form of the phrasal verbs from Exercise A.

I have a lot of personal rituals. Every night, I **(1)** _____ my closet and **(2)** _____ what I'm going to wear the next day. Then when I'm getting dressed in the morning, I always have to **(3)** _____ my socks first—I don't know why, but it's just what I do!

Also, I work from home, so in order to stay focused, I start each day by **(4)** _____ a list of things that I have to do that day. I feel a real sense of achievement when I **(5)** _____ the list at the end of the day and **(6)** _____ all the items I've managed to finish.

I'm also pretty neat—while I'm working, I usually **(7)** _____ my pens and pencils on my desk so that they are in a straight line. Sometimes I don't even notice that I'm doing it! And I can't bear a messy desk either—I have to **(8)** _____ my desk drawers at least once a week!

6 WRITING: avoiding run-on sentences

A Read this instant chat. Underline the run-on sentence in each post.

Earlier messages: 1 day 1 week 2 weeks 1 month 3 months 6 months 1 year **All**

Sarah says: 10:58
I just returned from a walk in the woods, every New Year's Day I put on my hiking boots and walk in the same place. I do this to think about the year that's passed and to make plans for the year ahead.

Joel says: 10:59
When my cat died, I planted a tree in my local park. I like it, it means I go back there every year on the anniversary of his death and remember him.

Gabriela says: 11:02
I have a personal ritual for when I'm worried, I buy a balloon. Then I write down my problem, tie it on the balloon, and let it go. As it goes into the sky, I allow it to take away my worries and cares.

Ana says: 11:03
When someone I love has a problem, I write them a letter. This reminds them that I'm thinking about them, it reminds them that they aren't going through life alone.

Spiros says: 11:05
I made an important promise ten years ago. Now, every morning, I remember my promise, I put on my ring. (It's my wedding ring!)

Edna says: 11:06
I loved reading this! There are some wonderful ideas here. I don't have any rituals, now I'll try to start one.

B Rewrite each sentence in Exercise A with a word or a punctuation mark from the box. Use each item only once.

| and because but when . ; |

1 Sarah: _____
2 Joel: _____
3 Gabriela: _____
4 Ana: _____
5 Spiros: _____
6 Edna: _____

skillsStudio

A »🎧 17 You will hear five short extracts in which people are talking about festivals in their country. Which festival is each speaker describing? Listen and match each picture with the correct speaker number.

B Listen again and match the verbs and phrasal verbs that you heard (1–8) with their definitions (a–h).

1 date back
2 honor
3 boost
4 pull in
5 maintain
6 turn up
7 hurl
8 generate

a) make something stay the same
b) throw
c) attract
d) began at a particular time in the past
e) arrive
f) help something to become more successful
g) make, create
h) respect for something

C Listen again. What does each speaker say about their festival? Write the correct letter next to each speaker. There are three extra letters that you do not need to use.

Speaker 1 ___

Speaker 2 ___

Speaker 3 ___

Speaker 4 ___

Speaker 5 ___

a) A festival held to honor an area's local industry
b) A festival you have to pay to attend
c) A relatively modern festival to draw visitors to the area
d) A festival to celebrate the historical importance of an animal
e) A ritual based on an ancient saying
f) A festival to mark the end of winter
g) A festival to promote marine conservation
h) A ritual whose origins are not certain

D Listen again and complete the table.

Speaker	Festival name	Country	Summary of how the festival is celebrated
1			
2			
3			
4			
5			

E Write a short description of about 250 words in your notebook about a ritual or festival that takes place in your country.

UNIT 7 DESIGNED TO PLEASE

1 VOCABULARY: design

A Put the letters into the correct order to make design words.

1 pot-yauliqt _____
2 peatmelt _____
3 unremuacaft _____
4 retaminui _____
5 quiune _____
6 envainitov _____
7 baforfalde _____
8 desporzaline _____

B Complete the text with the words from Exercise A.

LEARN PRODUCT DESIGN

Are you an inventor? Do you have a **(1)** _____ idea for a product: something that no one else has thought of before?

City Design College is offering a new course in product design. As part of the coursework, you'll learn how to turn ideas into real products using the **(2)** _____ new technology of 3D printing. You'll learn how to turn your drawings into a digital **(3)** _____ that can be used to print a **(4)** _____ model of your invention. The course will also teach you how to find factories abroad that can **(5)** _____ your product. Whether you want to make **(6)** _____ kitchen tools that will sell for a few dollars, or **(7)** _____ electronic devices that will sell for thousands, this course can help you get started. Our course is **(8)** _____ so that you are learning only the things you need to know, at a pace that is best for you.

2 GRAMMAR: possessive apostrophe

A Match each use of the possessive apostrophe with an example.

1 with a singular noun

2 with a plural noun

3 to show separate ownership

4 to show joint ownership

5 with two consecutive nouns

6 with a gerund

a) Viviane's and Tom's fashion shows were both at 8 last night.

b) Joe and Jenny's mother helped fund their first fashion collection.

c) Mark's design won first prize in a competition.

d) It was Colone's daughter's idea to make an all-pink collection.

e) The new collection's unveiling was the most exciting event of the year.

f) It was the fashion editors' favorite collection, but it sold poorly in stores.

B Choose the correct options to complete the sentences.

1 *Dolce and Gabbana's / Dolce's and Gabbana's* new collection might be the company's best ever.

2 It's terrible that designers use pink for *girl's / girls'* clothes and blue for *boy's / boys'* clothes.

3 The *company closing's / company's closing* will leave dozens of designers unemployed.

4 The company was named by combining the two *designers' mothers' / designer's mothers'* last names.

5 The *designer and CEO's / designer's and CEO's* ideas for the company often conflicted with each other.

WATCH OUT!

✗ He designs affordable, comfortable childrens' clothes.

✓ _____
_____

C Complete the text. Write an apostrophe (') or 's after the words. If nothing is needed, write X.

I had a billion-dollar idea!
POSTED, Tuesday, 11:24 p.m.

Tonight I was looking at celebrity pictures online and thought to myself, "I love that **(1)** star_____ shoes! Where can I get them?" Well, why isn't there a website for that? You should be able to click on **(2)** celebrities_____ **(3)** shoes_____ in a picture to find out where to buy them. My **(4)** sister_____ **(5)** husband_____ cousin is a computer programmer—maybe she can help me. She could handle the **(6)** site_____ programming, and I could do the design and talk to the shoe **(7)** companies_____. It's a great idea, isn't it? Everyone would like it—men and women, people who like **(8)** sneakers_____ and people who like high **(9)** heels_____. I'm sure **(10)** Adidas_____ and **(11)** Gucci_____ marketing departments would both love it. Just remember that it's my idea—don't try to steal it!

---

3 READING: inferring factual information

A Read the text. Check the statements that you can infer from the text.

1. ☐ The average person does not enjoy painting their home.
2. ☐ Only an expert can paint a room correctly.
3. ☐ Even a small amount of yellow paint can make some people angry.
4. ☐ Yellow would not be a good color for a baby's room.
5. ☐ People may sleep better in a blue room.
6. ☐ Red is a great color for rooms that host parties and big dinners.
7. ☐ It's a good idea to paint your bedroom red.
8. ☐ Green is a cheerful and relaxing color.

B Underline the words in the text that helped you infer the checked sentences in Exercise A.

Interior design pro tips: Get in the right mood with the right color

[1] If you're like most people, the thought of painting the walls doesn't exactly fill your heart with happiness and joy. But after the paint has dried, you want your new room to put you and your family in the right mood: cheerful in the kitchen, calm and relaxed in the bedroom, and ready to party in the living room. Experts say that the color you choose for your walls can have a real effect on the way you feel when you're in the room, so choose wisely. Here's a look at how different colors can affect your mood.

[2] **Yellow:** This is a cheerful color that reminds people of sunshine. If you want to feel energized, this is a great color for you, and is an excellent choice for dining room, bathrooms, and kitchens. However, a little yellow goes a long way. Large amounts of yellow can make people angry. Also, according to research, babies cry more in yellow rooms.

[3] **Blue:** Studies show that blue interiors can lower blood pressure and reduce your heart rate. For this reason, many people choose this relaxing color for their bedrooms. It's also great for living rooms and other places where you want to feel calm and serene.

Lighter shades of blue are best if this is the effect you want, as dark blue can actually make people feel depressed. However, light blue can also be quite a cold color, so make sure you add warmth to the room with furniture and fabrics.

[4] **Red:** Red is a great choice if you want to create an exciting atmosphere and get people talking. This color can make your heart beat faster, especially at night, and is great for living rooms and dining rooms. However, some people find it difficult to sleep well in a red room—something to remember when choosing colors for the bedroom.

[5] **Green:** This color brings together the best qualities of blue and yellow. You can paint nearly any room in the house green: kitchens, living rooms, and bedrooms. According to studies, people often feel more comfortable and less stressed in a green interior.

[6] **Orange:** This color gets people excited and energized. For this reason, experts say that this is a great color for an exercise room, but it is not recommended for living rooms or bedrooms.

4 VOCABULARY: phrasal verbs

A Complete the sentences with the words from the box.

off on out to up with

1 Is Victoria Beckham going to bring _____ a new collection this year?
2 When did Frank Gehry's career in architecture really take _____?
3 How did Jony Ive come up _____ the design for the iPod?
4 Does Zaha Hadid draw _____ her building designs herself?
5 Why do you think Prabal Gurung's designs have caught _____?
6 Do you think kids look up _____ designers?

B Choose the correct options to complete the article.

Jonathan Ive

Sir Jonathan Paul "Jony" Ive is an English designer and a top employee at Apple, Inc. When Apple first **(1)** *brought out / drew up* the iPod in 2001, many people gave credit to company founder Steve Jobs for **(2)** *looking up to / coming up with* the idea for the innovative device. However, it was Ive who **(3)** *drew up / took off* the first sketches of the music player. The iPod quickly **(4)** *caught on / brought out* with consumers, and Ive's career really **(5)** *caught on / took off*. Apple's success continued with the iPhone and iPad, both of which were designed by Ive. Young designers around the world **(6)** *come up with / look up to* Ive and he has received many awards. In 2004, the BBC named him the "Most Influential Person in British Culture" and in 2012 he was knighted by Princess Anne.

5 GRAMMAR: past perfect vs. past perfect progressive

A Complete each sentence with the past perfect or past perfect progressive form of the verbs from the box. Sometimes both verb forms are possible.

be come up with draw up end open wait

1 Because we were an hour late, the fashion show for the label's Autumn/Winter 2015 collection _____ before we arrived.
2 I _____ sample designs for two hours when the client finally turned up.
3 His design talent was clear from a young age. By the time he was 30, he _____ stores in Paris, London, and Tokyo.
4 Jorge _____ in New York City for a year when he met Mika during an interior design class.
5 We _____ for over an hour before the models and designers finally arrived.
6 Maria and Jim _____ design ideas for over a year when they decided to start their own company.

WATCH OUT!

(✗) She didn't show anyone her designs until she had been finishing them.

(✓) _____
_____

42

B Complete the text with the past perfect or past perfect progressive of the verbs from the box. Sometimes both forms are possible.

ask   attend   change   make   notice   think

The first automobile designer

When Harley Earl was born in 1893, his father owned a company called the Earl Carriage Works, which **(1)** _____ horse-drawn carriages for several years. By 1908, the company was making parts and accessories for cars and Earl's father **(2)** _____ the name of his company to Earl Automobile Works. Harley Earl began studying engineering at Stanford University, but he **(3)** _____ classes for only a short time when he decided to work for his father instead. He began designing cars and by 1926, the general manager of General Motors **(4)** _____ the Earls' designs and **(5)** _____ him to come to Detroit to design a new Cadillac. It was so successful that Earl was asked to become head of a new department called "the art and color section." This department produced some of the classic American cars of the 1950s, with fins and chrome. Earl is credited as the first designer to think of a car as a "concept" and a car design as a work of art. Before Harley, car designers **(6)** _____ very little about these things.

6 COMMUNICATION STRATEGY: distancing language

A Complete the conversation with the phrases from the box.

I wanted to suggest   I was hoping   I was thinking we   I was wondering

Jim: I want to paint the kitchen, and **(1)** _____ we could talk about the colors.

Nicole: Sure. **(2)** _____ might choose a neutral color, like cream.

Jim: Oh, really? **(3)** _____ using something more exciting.

Nicole: More exciting? Like what?

Jim: **(4)** _____ if we should paint it orange and red.

Nicole: Orange and red?! I'm not sure that's the best idea. Those colors don't really work with the table and chairs.

Jim: Yeah, I guess. Maybe cream is best, after all.

B 🎧 18 Listen and check your answers.

C Use the prompts to write requests and suggestions. Use distancing language.

1   I want / ask your opinion about / paint the bathroom blue

_____

2   I think / you should buy a new rug / match the color of the sofa

_____

3   I hope my mother / help us / by come up with an idea of how to decorate the baby's room

_____

4   I wonder / if Maria had any suggestions for an interesting design for the kitchen

_____

skillsStudio

A Read the newspaper article about a skyscraper in London. What is the purpose of the article?

1 to amuse readers with stories about the building's problems
2 to explain the mistakes in the building's design in detail
3 to allow the building's supporters and its critics to give their opinions
4 to propose a solution to the problems caused by the building

B Read the article again. Look at the words in bold and try to figure out what they mean. Then write the words from the box next to their definitions.

awning   context   dispute   gawk   glare   overcast   ray   scorch   spire   suspend

1 _____: to look at something for a long time, usually in surprise
2 _____: a serious disagreement that lasts for a long time
3 _____: a narrow line of light from the sun or a lamp
4 _____: the general situation in which something happens, which helps to explain it
5 _____: with a sky completely full of clouds
6 _____: the pointed top of a church tower or other building
7 _____: cloth hung above a window or door to protect against rain or sun
8 _____: an unpleasant bright light
9 _____: to officially stop something for a short time
10 _____: to burn something enough to damage it

C Read the article again. Write the number of the paragraph that ...

a) gives the writer's personal experience with the building. ____
b) says what the company that made the building is going to do. ____
c) gives examples of other buildings with similar problems. ____
d) explains how the building got its name. ____
e) gives an opinion of modern architecture in general. ____
f) talks about how the building has affected nearby businesses. ____

D You are the manager of a store affected by the "Walkie Scorchie." Write a letter of complaint to the developers explaining what your particular issue is and demand that they take action. Write about 200 words.

London's car-frying skyscraper

[1] London's skyline has a new addition this week: the Walkie Scorchie. Joining the crowded group of glass skyscrapers with nicknames such as the Shard, the Gherkin, and the Cheese grater, is 20 Fenchurch Street, which had previously been known as the Walkie Talkie, because it looked a little like a gigantic two-way radio. But the 37-story office building has gained some new nicknames: the death ray, the fryscraper, the Walkie Scorchie. This is because the building's south-facing side concentrates and reflects the sun's **rays** into an intense beam of light. Along a 30-yard stretch of sidewalk—not very far from where the Great Fire of 1666 started—London's burning.

[2] On Tuesday afternoon, I was sent out to see if I could fry an egg in the heat, a task that I thought was impossible on an  **overcast** September day. But, not only was it possible, I had to run out of the death ray that was slowly cooking my egg, because the thinning hairs on my head started to catch fire. On Monday, the air temperature in the concentrated beam reached 69.8° C (158° F). To put that in **context**, the world's hottest temperature was recorded in Death Valley, California, at 56.7° C (134° F) over 100 years ago. Dr. Simon Foster, a physicist, accidentally left his measuring equipment in a black bag on the sidewalk for 10 minutes on Tuesday. The thermometer read 92.6° C (198.7° F). "It's insane. It's just ridiculous. I've never felt heat like it," he says.

[3] But while the Walkie Scorchie is causing much amusement to curious pedestrians coming to **gawk**, it is causing serious problems for the row of shops caught in its **glare**. Ali Akay of Re-Style barbers, opposite the tower, told me he was "too stressed" to talk, but confirmed his carpet was burned on Tuesday and many of the plastic bottles of shampoo and hair gel in the window had started to melt. Diana Pham, assistant manager of the next-door Viet Cafe, admitted she was enjoying the extra business from office workers coming to get a little sunshine at lunchtime. But four tiles on the outside of her café have popped off the building in the last two days, and her furniture is starting to cook. "The chairs started to smell, very, very bad, like they were burning. We thought something terrible was happening," she says. At the end of last week, the side mirror and panels of a businessman's car had all melted, after being parked outside the café for just two hours. Parking has now been **suspended** on the street.

[4] The developers responsible for 20 Fenchurch Street say that the building's glass has been there for months, but only led to problems in the last few days, "caused by the current location of the sun in the sky." They promise they are working on a solution, which for now is likely to be a temporary **awning** to protect the shops.

[5] Architectural experts are not impressed and point out that too many modern skyscrapers are causing similar problems. Three years ago, residents at the Vdara hotel in Las Vegas—designed by the same architect as the Walkie Talkie—complained of being "scorched" by the rays hitting the swimming pool area. The rays were melting their plastic drinking cups, guests claimed. In Dallas, the Museum Tower, a 42-story apartment building, reflected so much light into the neighboring Nasher Sculpture Center that it threatened artworks in the gallery, **scorched** plants, and caused a two-year **dispute** between the two parties.

[6] For most of the Londoners in the area, however, the issue is not so much the heat being created, but the fact that a city full of masterpieces of traditional architecture is fast becoming a city of glass. As little as a decade ago, you could turn a corner and find a beautiful old **spire** amid the modern office towers. Now, your only guarantee is being blinded by the light.

Source: www.telegraph.co.uk

UNIT 8 A FAIR DEAL?

1 VOCABULARY: social issues

A 🎧 19 Listen and write the words you hear.

1 _____ 3 _____ 5 _____ 7 _____

2 _____ 4 _____ 6 _____ 8 _____

B Complete the sentences with words from Exercise A.

1 Samira is a _____—she had to leave her home country because of the war there.

2 There is a lot of _____ in this area because the unemployment rate is high and people don't have enough money to live on.

3 The group campaigns against _____ in the workplace and demands equality for all.

4 She's not only a successful singer, she's also an _____ for a children's charity.

5 All donations will go directly to _____ children to help give them a better start in life.

6 Xavier used his fortune to found a _____ organization, which helps unemployed young people to find work.

7 Sergio received funding for his Ph.D. from a scientific _____.

8 Aid workers have warned that the famine could become a _____ disaster.

2 GRAMMAR: *would rather* and *would prefer*

A Correct the mistakes in the sentences. Two sentences are correct.

1 Sam would prefer not take part in the demonstration tomorrow.

2 Theo would rather get involved in student politics.

3 They would prefer donations not to be send by mail.

4 He would rather people volunteered in the hospital shop.

5 We would rather she not to volunteer anywhere dangerous.

6 We'd prefer not collect donations until tomorrow.

> **WATCH OUT!**
>
> ⊗ I'd rather to donate time than money.
>
> ⊘ _____
> _____

B Complete the text with the verbs from the box in the correct form.

give   go   invest   not/receive   not/transport   see

EARTHQUAKE APPEAL

We're very grateful for the overwhelming response from the public to our earthquake appeal. We have plenty of canned food items now, so we would prefer (1) _____ any more. Instead we would rather people (2) _____ warm clothes or bedding. In addition, local hospitals have reported that their blood supplies are running low. If you are able to donate blood, doctors would rather you (3) _____ directly to Central Hospital because they would prefer (4) _____ the blood from regional clinics. We are also asking for donations of money to help with rebuilding the area. We would rather (5) _____ in projects that will benefit the local community far into the future, so we will be consulting with locals to find out where they would prefer (6) _____ the money spent.

3 LISTENING: for main ideas

A You are going to listen to a business studies lecture. Number these topics in the order you think the speaker will talk about them.

a) ____ the company's recent history

b) ____ the story of the company's beginning

c) ____ an overview of what the company does

B 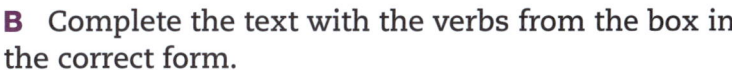20 Listen to the lecture and check your answers.

C Listen again. Choose the sentence that best expresses the main idea of each part.

Main idea 1:
a) The company sells jewelry, items for the home, toys, games, baskets, stationery, and many other things.
b) The company buys directly from producers at a fair price and sells through a number of different channels.
c) The company sells directly to customers at festivals.

Main idea 2:
a) Edna Ruth Byler was strongly affected by the situation of artisans in Puerto Rico in 1946, so she started a company to help them.
b) The name of Edna Ruth Byler's first company was the Overseas Needlepoint and Crafts Project.
c) Edna Ruth Byler is no longer involved in running the company.

Main idea 3:
a) The company turned 50 in 1996.
b) Ten Thousand Villages won an important award.
c) After 50 years in business, the company changed its name and expanded.

D Choose the correct options to complete the sentences.

1 Ten Thousand Villages *makes* / *doesn't make* a profit.
2 The artisans make handcrafted items and *sell* / *donate* them to Ten Thousand Villages.
3 Ten Thousand Villages sells the products in over *17* / *70* stores throughout the U.S.
4 Edna Ruth Byler came from *the U.S.* / *Puerto Rico*.
5 She started an organization called *Ten Thousand Villages* / *Overseas Needlepoint and Crafts Project*.
6 She bought products from artisans and sold them in *North America* / *developing countries*.
7 In 1996, the company was *30* / *50* years old.
8 The company started selling online in *1997* / *2006*.

4 VOCABULARY: social justice

A Match the sentences (1–6) with their same meanings (a–f).

1 Some governments provide *benefits* for people living in poverty. ___
2 Some countries *can't afford to* help their own citizens. ___
3 Governments *have a responsibility to* help people get work. ___
4 If you're poor, you *have the right to* government benefits. ___
5 Almost every country has citizens who don't have enough to *live on*. ___
6 Almost every country has *unemployed* people. ___

a) Leaders of countries *have an obligation to* help people find employment.
b) Poor people *are entitled to* receive money from the government.
c) There are *people who are out of work* all over the world.
d) In some countries, *money for the poor* is available from the government.
e) Everywhere, there are people who can't *manage to survive with what they have*.
f) Some governments *don't have enough money to* give to people who need it.

B Complete the ad with the correct form of the words and phrases from the box.

| benefits   can afford to   have a responsibility to |
| have the right to   live on   unemployed |

Everyone **(1)** _____ food, clothing, and shelter. But 842 million people in the world do not have enough to eat. Many of them go hungry because they **(2)** _____ buy enough food. Others don't have enough to eat because there simply isn't enough food available. Many of the world's hungry are **(3)** _____, and have no access to government **(4)** _____. If you have enough to eat, then you **(5)** _____ help those who do not. A donation of just a few dollars a day is enough to **(6)** _____ for someone in need.

Please give generously to Give Food Now.

5 GRAMMAR: noun clauses as subjects

A Write the letter of the correct form for each sentence.

a) Question word is the subject   b) Question word is the object

1 ___ What the government needs to do is provide better benefits.
2 ___ What's difficult to understand is the scale of the poverty.
3 ___ Who gains the most from this funding is debatable.
4 ___ How people donate money is not important.
5 ___ Where you decide to volunteer can make a big difference.
6 ___ What happens next is up to the locals of the region.

> **WATCH OUT!**
>
> ⊗ What does the charity need is …
>
> ✓ _____
>   _____

B Put the words in the correct order to make sentences.

1 themselves / feed / to / what / need / people / way / a / is

_____

2 the / who / receives / aid / uncertain / most / is

_____

3 donations / year / where / send / this / undecided / we / is

_____

4 we / distribute / is / food / what / do / of / baskets

_____

5 community / important / our / how / is / we / support

_____

6 donate / what's / to / directly / best / is / money

_____

6 WRITING: sentence variety

A Match each sentence (1–7) with a grammatical structure (a–g).

1 Seeing that news story made me sad.
2 Everyone has a responsibility to help others.
3 I want to get people to take the issue seriously.
4 If we work together, we can make a difference.
5 It's helpful to give even a small amount.
6 What I'd like to do is make it easier for people to give.
7 The donations, which I collect, are given to charity.

a) regular subject + verb + object sentence structure
b) noun clause as subject
c) gerund as subject
d) *It's* + adjective + infinitive
e) conditional
f) relative clause
g) causative (*have/get something done* or *have someone do/get someone to do something*)

B Rewrite sentences 1–6 from the paragraph, using the grammatical structures and prompts below.

Helping the homeless
close to home

(1) It may surprise you to discover how many homeless people there are in your area. (2) They really need your support to help them get back on their feet. (3) But knowing how to get involved in charity work is not always easy. (4) You could make a significant contribution by volunteering in some way. (5) Charities may be the main source of funding for local homeless shelters and often need volunteers. Or you could turn your hand to fundraising: (6) You could think of new and exciting ways of persuading people to donate money to the charity.

1 **gerund as subject:** Discovering _____.
2 **noun clause as subject:** What they really need _____.
3 ***It's* + adjective + infinitive:** But it's not always easy _____.
4 **conditional:** If you volunteer _____.
5 **relative clause:** Charities, _____,
  may be the main source of funding for local homeless shelters.
6 **causative:** You could think of new and exciting ways of _____.

skillsStudio

A Read the article and answer the question below.

Ben Affleck at the Senate in Washington

Actor and director Ben Affleck left Hollywood behind this week when he appeared at the Senate to talk to the Committee on Foreign Relations about violence in the Democratic Republic of Congo. Other celebrity humanitarians with good intentions have visited the Senate in the past, but have been unpersuasive when questioned by senators. Affleck, however, was knowledgeable about the subject and spoke well about the complex situation in the region. He outlined ways that the U.S. government could help, including increasing agricultural aid and guaranteeing fair elections. Affleck proved his commitment to the region in 2010 by setting up the Eastern Congo Initiative, a U.S.-based organization, which provides support and grants for people in eastern Congo. Affleck says that, apart from his family and his work, this is what he wants to be remembered for, so he takes it very seriously.

According to the article, why did Ben Affleck speak to the Senate Committee on Foreign Relations?

1 Because he wanted to show the U.S. government how it can help deal with violence in the Democratic Republic of Congo.
2 Because he wanted his Eastern Congo Initiative to be taken seriously.
3 Because he wanted to get the U.S. government to provide grants for his Eastern Congo Initiative.

B 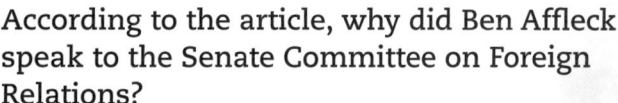 **21** Listen to a radio debate and answer these questions.

1 Which speaker thinks that celebrities' humanitarian efforts can do more good than harm?

_____

2 Which speaker thinks that celebrities' humanitarian efforts can do more harm than good?

_____

C Listen again and choose the correct answer.

1 Paul Cunard is a …
  a) radio host.
  b) journalist.
  c) representative of the Kitts Humanitarian Foundation.
2 Paul thinks that celebrities do charity work to …
  a) raise the profile of the charity.
  b) help poor people.
  c) make money for themselves.
3 Rosie argues that we shouldn't generalize about …
  a) celebrities' intentions.
  b) celebrities' profiles.
  c) the issues that celebrities care about.

4 Rosie thinks that celebrities may feel …
  a) a less strong sense of responsibility to help others than non-celebrities.
  b) a stronger sense of responsibility to help others than non-celebrities.
  c) just as strong a sense of responsibility to help others as non-celebrities.
5 Paul thinks that Live 8 was …
  a) about making money rather than tackling global poverty.
  b) controlled by the corporate sponsors.
  c) about getting governments to promise to deal with poverty.
6 Paul says that the sales of some of the Live 8 singers went up by … after the concert.
  a) 36,000%   b) 3,600%   c) 360%
7 Paul thinks that the presence of celebrities leads people to focus on … of problems.
  a) short-term symptoms and causes
  b) short-term causes rather than long-term symptoms
  c) short term symptoms rather than long-term causes

8 Rosie mentions Ben Affleck's Eastern Congo Initiative as an example of a celebrity who ….
  a) has raised awareness of a short-term crisis.
  b) is committed to addressing the long-term issues in a country.
  c) has used his charity to raise his profile.

D Listen again and match the words you heard in the debate (1–8) with their correct meanings (a–h).

1	representative (*n.*)	a)	public image
2	profile (*n.*)	b)	draw attention to
3	outweigh (*v.*)	c)	innocent, showing lack of experience
4	highlight (*v.*)	d)	establish, set up
5	found (*v.*)	e)	a group of people acting together, for example, in business
6	naïve (*adj.*)	f)	a person acting on behalf of someone or something
7	corporate (*adj.*)	g)	be more important than
8	sustainable (*adj.*)	h)	capable of being continued

E Listen again and complete the phrases you hear.

1 Would you like to _____ in here?
2 I _____ what you're saying.
3 Would you like to _____ to that?
4 I couldn't _____ more.
5 I see your _____.
6 We're just going to have to _____ to disagree on this.

F Write the numbers of the phrases from Exercise E next to their function.

a) To invite somebody to contribute to a conversation: ___, ___
b) To admit that something somebody else has said is true: ___, ___
c) To show that you don't agree with something: ___, ___

G Write an email of about 250 words to the radio station in response to the program, giving your opinion on the debate.

UNIT 9 COMPETITIVE EDGE

1 GRAMMAR: gerunds after prepositions

A Choose the correct options to complete the sentences.

1 People who worry *about* / *of* losing generally do not look forward *for* / *to* competing with others.
2 However, those who feel they are good *at* / *on* doing something are often excited *with* / *about* demonstrating their abilities in competitions.
3 If you are bored *for* / *by* exercising alone, you might enjoy a competitive sport like soccer or tennis.
4 It's not healthy for children to care *about* / *on* winning too much; they should only be interested *in* / *of* having fun and doing their best.
5 It's natural not to be happy *to* / *about* losing a game, but too many athletes today complain *about* / *for* losing because of decisions made by the referee.

WATCH OUT!

Ⓧ As a parent, I object to have beauty contests for children.

Ⓧ _____
_____

Ⓧ Would you like to playing soccer in the park on Sunday?

Ⓒ _____
_____
_____

B Complete the text with the correct form of the verb or adjective from the box.

| bored | capable | excited | happy | insist | interested | look | object | responsible |

This year's World Beard and Mustache Championships to be held in Portland, Oregon. Will you be there?

Mark Lewis
Check this out! I'm really **(1)** _____ forward to seeing this in September. Anyone else?

Jenny Vega
Yeah, I'm very **(2)** _____ in seeing this. Mark, you still have six months before the competition. Maybe you can grow a beard and enter the contest?

Mark Lewis
Ha ha! I'm not **(3)** _____ of growing a long beard in such a short time. Also, I think my girlfriend Lisa might **(4)** _____ to seeing it every day.

Lisa Green
Mark, if you **(5)** _____ on growing a beard, I won't mind. It's true that I'm not a fan of beards and I wouldn't be **(6)** _____ about looking at it every day, but, I think that after a few weeks you'd be **(7)** _____ with having it.

Mark Lewis
Lisa, really? OK, then I'm going to grow one. Wow, I'm pretty **(8)** _____ about doing this!

Jenny Vega
Uh-oh. Sorry, Lisa, I guess I'm **(9)** _____ for starting this!

 Like   Share

2 READING: understanding text organization

A Read the text about the science of competition. What two things does it say about people who feel very worried in stressful situations?

a) Scientists are developing a chemical that will help them.
b) They may have a gene that makes them worry.
c) They always score lower on important exams.
d) With the right attitude, they can perform very well.

The Science of Competition

[1] From soccer games to corporate boardrooms, what helps us win? In their new book, Top Dog: The Science of Winning and Losing, bestselling authors Po Bronson and Ashley Merryman investigate the science behind competition.

[2] Most of us feel anxious before stressful situations **(1)** such as exams, job interviews, or sports competitions. Knowing the importance of the moment, our heart rate increases, our palms sweat, and our knees go weak. However, there are also people who simply don't feel stressed. Why? Genetics, say the experts. In stressful situations, the body produces a brain chemical called dopamine. Some people have methionine, **(2)** a special kind of gene that makes the brain reabsorb dopamine more slowly. In a stressful situation, **(3)** people who have the gene have a flood of dopamine in the brain, creating the sensation of worry.

[3] "The nickname for people with this gene is the worriers," Merryman explains. "In periods of stress … they have that flood of dopamine to the brain, and the brain just sort of shuts down."

[4] If you're a worrier, don't lose hope. Merryman says that your brain can adjust to routine stress— **(4)** in other words, you can thrive in high-pressure situations as long as they're familiar to you.

[5] A small change in attitude can also help worriers succeed. In a recent study, scientists focused on two groups of Harvard students taking the GREs, the American graduate school entrance exam. Before the test, researchers told one group of students that anxiety could actually improve their performance. Those students scored 50 points higher on a practice exam, and 65 points higher on the actual test.

[6] So if you're someone who doesn't perform well in stressful situations, just remember this experiment. You can work on processing information in ways that increase your chances of success.

Adapted from WGBH's "Innovation Hub"

B Look at the underlined phrases in the article. Write the number of the phrase that answers the questions.

a) What is methionine and what does it do? ___
b) How does dopamine affect some people in stressful situations? ___
c) According to the article, what are some examples of stressful situations? ___
d) How can the brain adjust to stress? ___

C Look at the underlined phrases in the article. Which phrase or phrases …

a) define a word or say what something is? ___
b) explain how something happens? ___ ___
c) give examples of something? ___

3 VOCABULARY: expressions of emotion

Complete the comments on the article in Section 2 with the words from the box.

| a desire to   a feeling of   the agony of   the fun of   the will to |

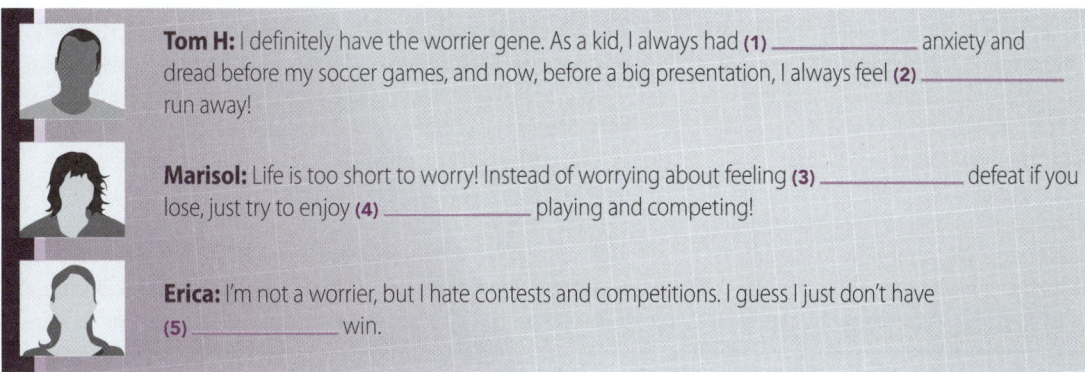

Tom H: I definitely have the worrier gene. As a kid, I always had **(1)** _____ anxiety and dread before my soccer games, and now, before a big presentation, I always feel **(2)** _____ run away!

Marisol: Life is too short to worry! Instead of worrying about feeling **(3)** _____ defeat if you lose, just try to enjoy **(4)** _____ playing and competing!

Erica: I'm not a worrier, but I hate contests and competitions. I guess I just don't have **(5)** _____ win.

4 GRAMMAR: verb + gerund

A Find and correct the five mistakes in the paragraph.

Every evening, millions of families around the world sit at home watch reality TV. We know we shouldn't waste time to watch the programs, but we have a good time laugh at them. They're harmless fun. Or are they? According to a recent survey of girls aged 11–17, those who like to watch reality TV are more competitive than those who don't. They are more likely to agree with statements such as, "You have to lie to get what you want," "I have a hard time to trust other girls," and "It's normal for girls to gossip and compete with each other." However, the effects of reality TV were not all negative. Sixty-two percent of the girls who watched reality TV said they found themselves to learn about new things and important issues.

WATCH OUT!

❌ Olympic athletes spent years prepare for this opportunity.

✓ _____

B Complete the paragraphs with the correct form of the words from the box.

find   have trouble   listen   perform   sit   solve   spend   think

If you **(1)** _____ relaxing during high-pressure events, you may benefit from positive visualization. The technique is simple. In the days before the event, close your eyes for a few minutes and imagine **(2)** _____ successfully. You can do it anywhere, but it is best to lie down in a comfortable place **(3)** _____ to gentle music. If you **(4)** _____ a few minutes a day visualizing, you will probably feel calmer and more confident on the day of the event. For many, it's a favorite Sunday ritual **(5)** _____ at the kitchen table doing the crossword puzzle.

You can **(6)** _____ people working on crosswords everywhere—crosswords even on the beach. If you love crosswords and have no difficulty **(7)** _____ the most challenging ones, you may want to enter the annual American Crossword Puzzle Tournament. At the three-day event, the world's best "solvers" compete for a $5,000 prize. Because they can't waste time **(8)** _____ of the answers, competitors often prepare by memorizing clues and answers from old puzzles.

5 VOCABULARY: scientific nouns and verbs

Choose the correct options to complete the text.

Is it *healthy* to be *competitive?*

Competitive or easygoing—which type are you? Why does it matter? (1) *Research / Theory* in the 1950s (and through the 1970s) seemed to **(2)** *measure / prove* that competitive Type A personalities had a higher risk of heart attacks and heart disease than Type Bs. This supported the common stereotype of the competitive business executive who rushes around, working late hours, until he finally has a heart attack. (The early **(3)** *theories / studies* were all done on men, by the way).

After **(4)** *researching / proving* the issue more, however, many experts now doubt the original **(5)** *conclusions / measurements*. They now think that only some parts of the Type A personality are connected with heart attacks: hostility, aggression, and difficulty expressing positive emotions.

This has led scientists to develop a new **(6)** *theory / measurement*. Perhaps the aggressive Type As have a higher risk of heart disease because they try to do everything themselves and become too stressed? They are not good team players and rarely let others help them. They also have trouble reducing stress because they are not good at expressing their emotions. In future **(7)** *experiments / conclusions*, researchers may want to examine the hearts of Type A people more closely. This will help them **(8)** *experiment / measure* their risk of heart attacks more accurately. For now, if you are a Type A personality, it is probably a good idea to be **(9)** *tested / experimented* for heart problems.

6 COMMUNICATION STRATEGY: paraphrasing

A **Read this text and choose the best paraphrases for the underlined sentences.**

1 **a)** Many people think that winning or losing in "Rock, Paper, Scissors" is mostly about luck.

 b) Everyone thinks that winning in the game is all about luck.

2 **a)** The most frequent opening gesture is "rock," according to statistics.

 b) Statistics show that players with less experience usually begin a game by playing the "rock" gesture.

3 **a)** You should play scissors first to beat experienced players because they'll know the tactic and will begin with paper.

 b) If you are playing an experienced opponent who already knows this strategy, begin by playing scissors because your experienced opponent will begin with paper.

4 **a)** The other player will probably make a different gesture the third time because they think this will be more difficult to predict.

 b) So that you can't guess what play they will make, your opponent won't make the same gesture three times in a row.

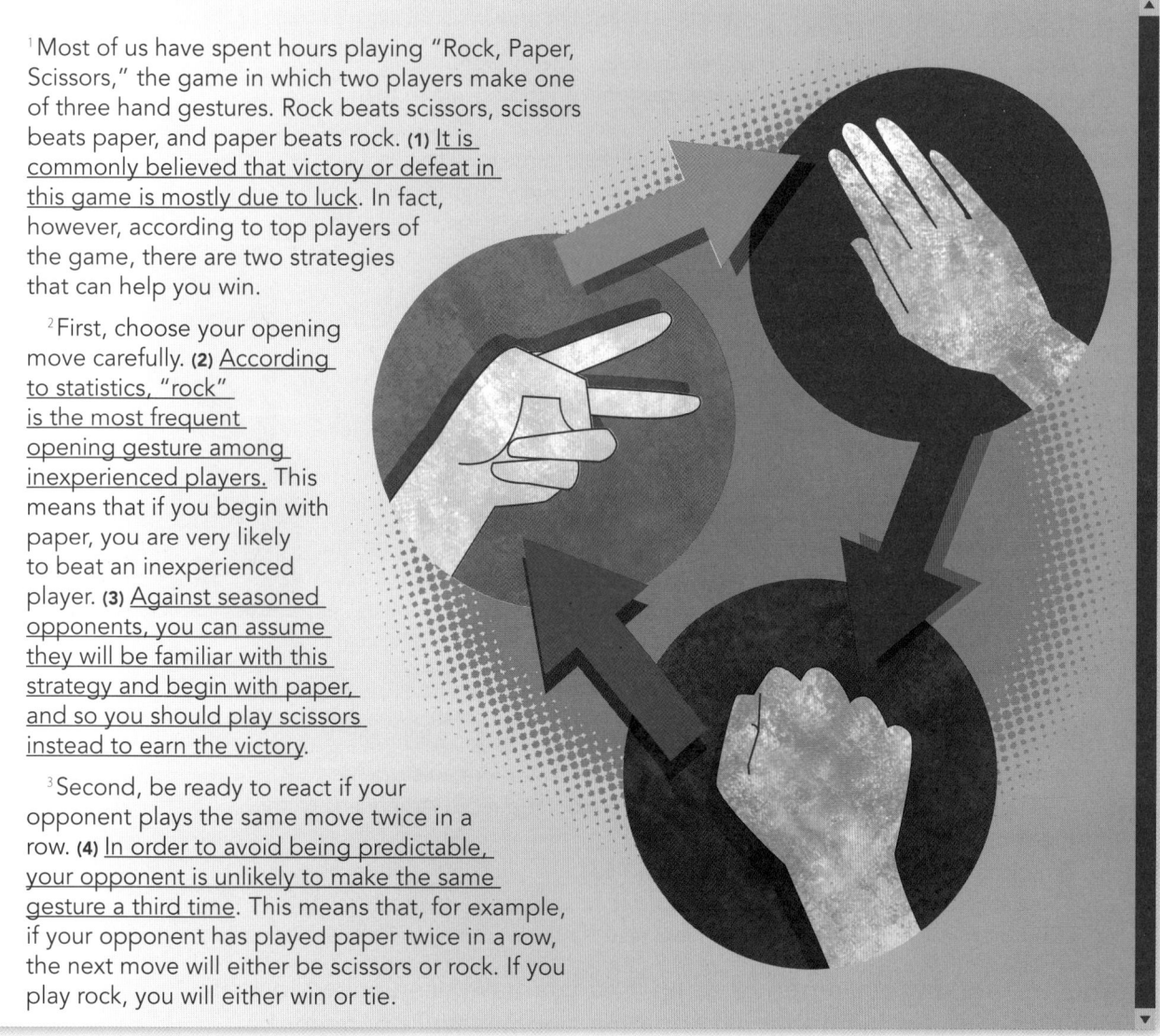

¹Most of us have spent hours playing "Rock, Paper, Scissors," the game in which two players make one of three hand gestures. Rock beats scissors, scissors beats paper, and paper beats rock. **(1)** <u>It is commonly believed that victory or defeat in this game is mostly due to luck</u>. In fact, however, according to top players of the game, there are two strategies that can help you win.

²First, choose your opening move carefully. **(2)** <u>According to statistics, "rock" is the most frequent opening gesture among inexperienced players.</u> This means that if you begin with paper, you are very likely to beat an inexperienced player. **(3)** <u>Against seasoned opponents, you can assume they will be familiar with this strategy and begin with paper, and so you should play scissors instead to earn the victory</u>.

³Second, be ready to react if your opponent plays the same move twice in a row. **(4)** <u>In order to avoid being predictable, your opponent is unlikely to make the same gesture a third time</u>. This means that, for example, if your opponent has played paper twice in a row, the next move will either be scissors or rock. If you play rock, you will either win or tie.

B 🔊 **22** **Listen to two friends discussing the story, and check your answers to Exercise A.**

skillsStudio

A Read the opinion article from a news site. Which of the following best describes the author's opinion?

a) American methods to increase children's self-esteem are not working.

b) Americans should spend less money on trophies and give every child a less-expensive prize.

c) Americans must stop rewarding all children equally so they will be prepared for global competition.

B Read the article again. Choose the correct answers.

1 The author believes the world is more competitive now because …
   a) the quality of foreign universities has increased in the last generation.
   b) people all over the world compete for the same jobs and university places.
   c) more American children are playing competitive soccer.
   d) American private school students have improved their grades.

2 The word *intense* (line 16) means …
   a) emotional. b) global. c) expensive. d) extreme.

3 Why does the author think that American students are doing worse than students from other countries?
   a) Because many American schools do not give students low grades.
   b) Because some American schools give awards to every student.
   c) Because American students do worse on international tests.
   d) Because poor grades have hurt American students' self-esteem.

4 If you are *motivated* (line 69) to do something, you …
   a) are very good at it.
   b) have a strong desire to do it.
   c) are required to do it.
   d) feel afraid to do it.

5 Why does the author believe it is bad to give trophies to every child? Choose two reasons from the article.
   a) It does not prepare them for competition in the future.
   b) It unfairly makes winners experience the agony of defeat.
   c) It puts too much importance on hard work instead of creativity.
   d) It actually hurts self-esteem instead of improving it.

C Look at the statements. Write T (true), F (false), or NM (not mentioned).

1 ___ At the University of Washington, 18% of students come from China.

2 ___ Many foreign students have wealthier families than American students.

3 ___ Soccer teams give trophies to everyone to encourage more Americans to try the sport.

4 ___ American youth soccer organizations spend $3 billion each year on trophies.

5 ___ Many American children are now ashamed to receive a "B" grade in school.

6 ___ According to Carol Dweck, children feel less confident if they are praised too much.

D You are working at a summer camp, and you have been asked to write to parents to inform them that participation trophies will no longer be given to each child. Write a letter of about 200 words explaining the change and the reasons for it.

When everyone gets a trophy, *who really wins?*

Today's American children are going to be entering a world that is more competitive than ever. Thanks to globalization and the internet, the job vacancies of the future will be able to be filled by any applicant, anywhere in the world. But that's not all. Today's high school students will have to compete with the rest of the world not just for a job, but also for a place in an American university. This trend has already started: students from foreign countries make up 18% of the University of Washington's class of 2015. Most of them are from China. Wealthy Chinese families (often far wealthier than a typical American family) are even sending their children to expensive private elementary and secondary schools in the U.S. to give them an even bigger advantage.

Clearly, in order to succeed in the future, young Americans need to know that they will be facing intense competition, and they need to be prepared for it. But sadly, right now, we are telling them just the opposite. In an attempt to build young people's self-esteem, competition has been almost totally removed from American schools and sports. A generation ago, only the winners received a trophy. Now, everyone gets a trophy. Although we have developed this culture with the best intentions—we want our children to feel happy and confident, not sad and discouraged —the evidence suggests that our actions are not having the desired effect. Instead, our children are less prepared, and more insecure, than ever before.

Youth soccer is a classic example of the way Americans reward children now. In most places, every player on every team receives a trophy just for participating, whether they win or lose. According to researcher Ashley Merryman, a single youth soccer league in California gave its young players over 3,500 awards in one year. Every child got an award, of course, and about one-third of them received at least two. Merryman also found that Americans now spend over $3 billion a year on trophies, mostly for children, and American youth soccer organizations spend over 12% of their budgets on trophies.

American schools have the same culture. One study found that 43% of American college students receive "A" grades (the highest possible grade in a scale from A to F). In American private schools, 86% of students are given only "A" or "B" grades. Elementary schools now often give end-of-year awards to each and every student—in alphabetical order, so everyone feels equal. However, while everyone is busy feeling good about themselves, international achievement tests show that American students continue to fall behind students in Europe, Asia, and elsewhere. According to the latest test results, U.S. students were not in the top half of countries for math, and just barely in the top half for reading and science. They were ranked far behind less wealthy countries such as Vietnam, Portugal, and Slovenia.

Our "everyone gets a trophy" culture is bad in two ways. First, it does not prepare children to face the fierce competition of the future. If they never experience the agony of defeat as young people, they may not be mentally strong enough to handle it as adults. Although failure can be difficult and painful for young people to experience, it also builds character. People who can recover from losing are more likely to succeed in the future.

Second, research suggests that giving trophies to everyone doesn't actually build self-esteem, but in fact damages it. Numerous studies show that children are not fooled when they receive awards simply for participating; they realize that they did not earn the honor and, as a result, they actually feel less confident. Columbia University professor Carol Dweck, an expert on self-esteem, has also found that when children are praised too much they are less motivated to work hard, and give up more easily when things are difficult. For these reasons, it's time to put away the trophies and start teaching young people the value of hard work and persistence.

UNIT 10 RISKY BUSINESS

1 VOCABULARY: safety and risk

A 🎧 **23** Listen and write the words or phrases you hear.

1 _____   5 _____
2 _____   6 _____
3 _____   7 _____
4 _____   8 _____

B Complete the sentences with the correct form of the words or phrases from Exercise A.

1 Theo would like to have the _____ of working for himself, but he needs the _____ of a steady job right now.

2 Starting my own business was _____, but I _____ and now it's really successful.

3 I think that if you _____ risk at an early age, then you're less likely to _____ when you grow up.

4 Jan _____ take on the new challenge and didn't let her fear of _____ stop her.

2 GRAMMAR: expressing ability

A What form goes after these verbs? Write *I* (infinitive), *B* (base form), or *G* (gerund) for each verb.

1 be good at ___   6 could/couldn't ___
2 (not) succeed in ___   7 be unable ___
3 (not) manage ___   8 be able ___
4 can/can't ___   9 be capable of ___
5 be incapable of ___

B Choose the correct options to complete the text.

Wing walking—not an easy sport at all
Posted by Pete209   May 05   02 Comments   [SHARE]   [SUGGESTIONS]

Expert wing walkers manage **(1)** _____ death-defying stunts for millions of spectators below. How do they do it? Well, they have to be good at **(2)** _____ their nerves, be capable of **(3)** _____ on a wing while doing stunts, be able **(4)** _____ their emotions, and succeed in **(5)** _____ their balance in strong winds. Oh, and they have to be able **(6)** _____ heights. It's pretty easy, really. Could you **(7)** _____ it, do you think? :-)

1 a) to perform   b) perform   c) performing
2 a) to overcome   b) overcome   c) overcoming
3 a) to balance   b) balance   c) balancing
4 a) to control   b) control   c) controlling
5 a) to keep   b) keep   c) keeping
6 a) to cope with   b) cope with   c) coping with
7 a) to do   b) do   c) doing

WATCH OUT!
✗ You have to be capable of take risks to run your own business.

✓ _____
_____

3 WRITING: requesting action

A Read the letter. Choose the function of each paragraph.

1 a) describe a problem   b) make suggestions   c) complain about the site
2 a) make suggestions   b) state requests   c) express confidence
3 a) thank the recipient   b) explain a problem   c) show trust in the recipient

---

Dear Mr. Fielder,

(1) We are writing to bring your attention to a problem we noticed at the adventure site recently constructed at Oldham Park. The teenagers who use the tower there often fool around and push each other off the platform. They could easily injure themselves or each other.

(2) We would like you to consider making the following changes to the adventure site:

- Place rubber on the laminated wood to prevent slipping.
- Place rubber on the ground below the platform to prevent injury to those landing on the ground.

(3) We would like to mention that we are happy with the adventure site. Since it was built, our teenagers have spent a lot of time outdoors. However, we feel that the suggestions above would reduce the risks of injury. We know we can count on you for prompt action.

Sincerely,

Peter Barker

on behalf of The Oldham Park Residents Committee

B Find expressions in the letter in Exercise A that have the same meaning as the sentences below. Write them next to the sentence.

a) We want you to think about … _____

b) We want to tell you about something we are aware of … _____

c) We know you'll do something about it quickly. _____

d) We want to say that we like … _____

C Number the paragraphs in the letter in the correct order. Then complete the letter with the answers from Exercise B.

Dear Mrs. Carter,

☐ **(1)** _____ the decision to install an elevator in the shopping mall because it is very useful for elderly people like myself and saves us having to climb the stairs!

(2) _____

☐ **(3)** _____ taking the following action:

- Close off the elevator so that children can't play on it.
- Fix the elevator as soon as possible.

☐ **(4)** _____ in the new shopping mall— the elevator is broken and children were playing on it, which is dangerous.

Sincerely,

Jody Hills

4 VOCABULARY: expressions with *risk*

A Match the words and phrases (1–6) with their definitions (a–f).

1	risk your life	a)	a study of the dangers or hazards
2	risky	b)	in danger
3	at risk	c)	do something that involves danger
4	risk assessment	d)	dangerous, hazardous
5	run the risk	e)	make the dangers smaller in size or number
6	reduce the risks	f)	do something that is so dangerous you might die

B Complete the blog with the correct form of the words and expressions from Exercise A.

HOME FOOTBALL SOCCER TENNIS GOLF BASEBALL AUTO RACING BASKETBALL **OTHER SPORTS**

All Sports *Blog*

NEWS
FEATURES
OPINION
VIDEOS
BLOG
PODCAST

Pages (3) 1 2 3 4 5

BASE jumping: too dangerous?

Marie101
member
since 2008

08:44

People **(1)** _____ every day to do dangerous sports. I mean, BASE jumping off buildings is so **(2)** _____ that it's illegal in most countries. There would be no point in carrying out a **(3)** _____ of this sport because it would be off the scale! Maybe if more BASE jumpers wore helmets, it would **(4)** _____ of injury?

JJracer
moderator

08:58

I doubt it. People would still **(5)** _____ of dying even if more of them wore helmets. They're selfish people. They put other people's lives **(6)** _____ because if they get into trouble, then somebody has to come out and rescue them.

5 GRAMMAR: past modals of deduction

A What is the function of these modal verbs? Write *SP* (strong probability), *MP* (moderate probability/improbability), or *SI* (strong improbability) for each modal verb.

1 couldn't have ___
2 might (not) have ___
3 must have ___

4 may (not) have ___
5 can't have ___

6 must not have ___
7 could have ___

B Choose the correct options to complete the text.

How did the magician Harry Houdini manage to escape from handcuffs?
In the 1920s, no one had seen escape artists like Houdini before. It
(1) *may have / must have* looked like magic. Of course, now we know that
he **(2)** *couldn't have / might have* used special powers. So how did he do it?
We don't know. Some people think that he **(3)** *may have / may not have*
been helped by someone, which is possible. Many modern magicians hide
a key between their teeth. Houdini **(4)** *might not have / could have* done
that, too. A few people think that he **(5)** *couldn't have / might have* opened
the lock from memory, but that seems unlikely. Whatever his secret, it
(6) *must have / may have* been an incredible sight!

WATCH OUT!

✗ He couldn't think it was
risky, or he wouldn't have
done it.

✓ _____
_____
_____

C Complete the conversation with the correct form of the
verbs in parentheses.

Al: Wow, you ran a risk there! Riding that elephant **(1)** _____ (*can't/be*)
very safe. You **(2)** _____ (*might/fall off*).

Maya: Well, you risked your life when you went on that camel! It **(3)** _____
(*might/throw*) you off! You **(4)** _____ (*could/have*) a terrible accident.

Sue: Well, I think you're both crazy. It **(5)** _____ (*may/seem*) risky at the
time, but you **(6)** _____ (*could/be*) seriously injured.

6 LISTENING: rapid speech

A 🎧 24 Listen to the conversation and complete the sentence.

The two friends are discussing …
1 the care that the boy with the broken arm received after his accident.
2 whether children should take risks when they play.
3 how parents should always take responsibility for their children's injuries.

B Listen to the conversation again and choose T (true)
or F (false).

1 The recreation area of the park has been closed off.
   T / F
2 The boy broke his arm when the slide collapsed on top of him.
   T / F
3 Mae thinks that children learn important skills by taking risks.
   T / F
4 Dave doesn't have children.
   T / F

C Listen to the conversation again. Complete the
phrases you hear.

1 _____ you hear that they've closed off …?
2 … they _____ decided that it's unsafe.
3 You've _____ be kidding.
4 It's _____ extreme.
5 I think parents just _____ keep …
6 I _____ about that.
7 That kid _____ fallen out of bed …
8 You've _____ point.

skillsStudio

A 🎧 **25** Guess the answers to these questions. Then listen to a talk by Joe Scott and check your answers.

1 Mount Kangchengjunga is the *second* / *third* highest mountain in the world.
2 It's on the border of India and *Nepal* / *Pakistan*.
3 It was first climbed in *1855* / *1955* by a team of British climbers.

B Choose the best summary of Joe's talk.

Joe's talk is about …
1 climbing Mount Kangchengjunga and what his next expedition will be.
2 his most recent expedition and his motivation for climbing mountains.
3 how dangerous it is to climb Mount Kangchengjunga.

C Listen again and write the topics in the order you hear them talked about.

☐ Joe's climb up Mount Kangchengjunga
☐ Facts and figures about Mount Kangchengjunga
☐ Joe's plans for the future
☐ The dangers associated with Mount Kangchengjunga
☐ The reasons why Joe loves to climb

D Listen and match the words that you heard (1–6) with their correct definitions (a–f).

1 a summit (*n.*)
2 sacred (*adj.*)
3 an avalanche (*n.*)
4 a thrill-seeker (*adj.*)
5 reckless (*adj.*)
6 rewarding (*adj.*)

a) a fall of snow down a mountain
b) without caring about danger
c) the highest point
d) providing personal satisfaction
e) someone who enjoys risky activities
f) holy or connected to religion

E Complete the sentences with a word or a short phrase.

1 Joe starts by asking the audience to _____ if they know something about Mount Kangchengjunga.

2 Mount Kangchengjunga is _____ high and is the _____ highest mountain in the world.

3 Mount Everest and K2 are both _____ than Mount Kangchengjunga, but Joe thinks that Mount Everest is _____ to climb than Mount Kangchengjunga.

4 Joe went up the _____ face of the mountain.

5 Joe thinks that the most dangerous things for climbers of Kangchengjunga are _____.

6 _____ of the mountaineers who have tried to climb Kangchengjunga have died in the attempt.

7 Joe _____ that extreme sportspeople must be risk-takers.

8 Joe describes his most recent climb as one of the most _____ of his life.

F Read the quote below. In your notebook write an opinion essay of about 300 words. Explain what you think Mark Zuckerberg means. Do you agree or disagree with this opinion?

"The biggest risk is not taking any risk." (Mark Zuckerberg)

UNIT 11 THROUGH THE LENS

1 READING: understanding text organization

A Read and complete the text with the sentences A–F. There is one extra sentence that you do not need to use.

A This means that the researchers considered the artistic intentions of each individual image as well as analyzing the overall trends and patterns that emerged according to location.

B This includes an essay about "Imagined Data Communities" by Nadav Hachman, and a blog "Gender, Age, and Ambiguity of Selfies on Instagram" by Mehrdrad Yazdani.

C So, overall, women clearly take significantly more selfies than men.

D This theory turned out to be true in the Selfiecity findings—Bangkok had the youngest subjects with an average age of 21.0 years and New York City was the oldest city with an average age of 25.3 years.

E One example of this is that women struck more extreme poses than men—the average amount of head tilt for women was 50% higher than for men (12.3° instead of 8.2°).

F Surprisingly though, only 3–5% of the pictures examined turned out to be selfies.

[1] Recent research has revealed some interesting trends in selfies taken in different parts of the world. Selfiecity is a project that was led by Dr. Lev Manovich and Software Studies Initiative. It set out to investigate the style of selfies taken in five different cities: Bangkok, Berlin, Moscow, New York City, and São Paulo. They randomly selected 120,000 pictures (20,000–30,000 per city) from a total of 656,000 images collected on Instagram and analyzed them to see if they were selfies. Given that everyone everywhere is talking about selfies right now, you might expect the percentage of selfies to be very high. **(1)** ___ The selfies that were selected for this research project were treated as a form of self-expression as well as a shared social experience. **(2)** ___

[2] The selfies were analyzed in various ways including the age, gender, mood, and poses of the subjects of the selfies. It is generally accepted that most selfies are taken by young people, particularly the under 30s. **(3)** ___ The average age of men was higher than that of women in every city. There was one trend that was true in all cities—the proportion of women in the selfies. In Bangkok 55.2% were women, in Berlin 59.4% were women, in New York City 61.6% were women, in São Paulo 65.4% were women, and in Moscow an enormous 82.0% of the selfies were of women! **(4)** ___ In terms of mood, the study also revealed that people from Bangkok smiled the most often, while people in Moscow smiled the least.

[3] More in-depth analysis of Selfiecity's findings is available on their website. **(5)** ___ In addition, visitors to the site can navigate through some of the selfies either by searching the different cities, or by examining specific characteristics of the subjects. Whatever the future holds for selfies, this project represents a fascinating snapshot of the kinds of selfies that are being taken around the world right now.

Source: http://selfiecity.net/#

B What are the functions of the sentences that were missing in Exercise A?

Which sentence …

1 summarizes what comes before it? ___
2 presents a further explanation of an important idea? ___
3 provides evidence against a point of view mentioned? ___
4 provides evidence in support of a claim? ___
5 gives specific examples of something mentioned? ___

2 VOCABULARY: describing pictures

Complete the texts with words or phrases from the box.

> background   foreground   in focus   landscape   left-hand side   out of focus
> portrait   right-hand side   subject

This picture is a beautiful **(1)** _____ of a lake in Banff National Park in Canada. It's easy to understand why the photographer chose this location as the **(2)** _____ of his picture. The mountains are stunning, and along with their reflection in the lake, are the first things you see. But if you look a little longer, you notice the forest on the **(3)** _____ and the cabin in the **(4)** _____ on the **(5)** _____.

This is a great **(6)** _____ of a little boy—it makes you wonder what he's thinking about. I really like the way that the trees in the **(7)** _____ are **(8)** _____ while the boy is **(9)** _____. It draws your attention to his face and his expression.

3 VOCABULARY: making comparisons

Choose the correct options to complete the conversation.

Marios: Which picture do you think I should submit for the photography competition?

Lianne: Wow, two completely different options!

Marios: Not totally—the pictures are **(1)** *similar in that* / *in contrast* they are both portraits.

Lianne: Yes, that's true. But I think the **(2)** *similarities* / *differences* end there! Because the subject in this picture looks happy, **(3)** *whereas* / *alike* this woman looks so sad.

Marios: Which do you prefer?

Lianne: Well, I don't think the picture of the boy really grabs your attention, **(4)** *alike* / *unlike* the one of the woman, which is very intriguing. What's more, although the angle from which the pictures were taken is **(5)** *similar* / *difference*, the picture of the woman is much more atmospheric.

Marios: That's interesting. Also, the background of the picture of the woman is out of focus, **(6)** *while* / *point of difference* the picture of the boy is perfectly in focus. OK then. I'm going to submit the one of the woman!

Lianne: Good luck!

4 GRAMMAR: connectors of addition / cause and effect

A Match (1–2) with (a–b) to make complete sentences.

1 Connectors of addition are used to … ___

2 Connectors of cause and effect are used to … ___

a) show how one thing makes another happen, or how one thought follows logically from another.

b) add further points or to provide more information in support of a point.

B For each connector, write A (addition) or C (cause and effect).

1 also ___
2 and ___
3 as a result of ___
4 besides that ___
5 as a consequence ___
6 moreover ___
7 because ___

8 due to ___
9 in addition to ___
10 therefore ___
11 so ___
12 because of ___
13 furthermore ___

C Choose the correct options to complete the text.

August 29 by Joanne Tanner   8 comments

Blog question: Is thinner always better?

Share   Report   Comment   Next post ▶

Weight loss apps: Do they really work?

The current craze for selfies seems to be having an effect on body image **(1)** *so / because* people are constantly comparing themselves to their peers. **(2)** *Due to / As a consequence*, we've seen the emergence of new apps, which have been designed to take 10 or 15 pounds off your weight in pictures. **(3)** *Moreover, / So,* I decided to take a look at one of these apps myself so that I could see what all the hype was about. I installed the app, and then I took a quick picture of myself **(4)** *also / because* the app only works on selfies. I decided to see what I would look like if I was 15 pounds lighter—the results were not good. I looked sick **(5)** *besides that / because of* my incredibly thin face. My cheekbones were too sharp and my forehead looked huge. **(6)** *In addition to / As a consequence* that, my ears were out of proportion with my face! **(7)** *Moreover, / Therefore,* I can guarantee that thinner is not always better, and I have since deleted the app from my phone!

WATCH OUT!

✗ Lots of people want to be thinner as a result selfies.

✓ _____
_____
_____

5 COMMUNICATION STRATEGY: making comparisons

A Match (1–8) with (a–h) to make complete sentences.

1 In the first picture, the subject is smiling, …
2 Both pictures are alike …
3 The first picture looks professional, …
4 Another point of difference is …
5 The first picture is very bright and …
6 The pictures are similar in that …
7 The first picture was taken in a city, …
8 One similarity is that both …

a) pictures were taken outside.
b) whereas in the second, the subject looks serious.
c) the angle from which the picture was taken.
d) unlike the second, which was taken in a forest.
e) while the second looks like an amateur effort.
f) because they both show people playing sports.
g) both were taken during the day.
h) in contrast, the second is dark.

B Write the sentence numbers from Exercise A in the correct place.

1 To explain a similarity between two things: ___, ___, ___

2 To explain a difference between two things: ___, ___, ___, ___, ___

C »♪26 Listen to a man comparing the two pictures. Write *S* if he describes a similarity and *D* if he describes a difference.

1 ___   5 ___
2 ___   6 ___
3 ___   7 ___
4 ___   8 ___

A

B

6 GRAMMAR: verb + gerund/infinitive with a change in meaning

A Match the sentences (1–10) with their correct definitions of the words in bold (a–j).

1 I **forgot to turn** the lights out.
2 I **forgot meeting** her last summer.
3 We **regret to inform** you that the plane is delayed.
4 Sue **regrets introducing** her boyfriend to her parents.
5 I must **remember to buy** a present for my mother.
6 Do you **remember buying** this coat?
7 Should we **stop to have** lunch?
8 I'm going to **stop eating** chocolate in January.
9 I'll **try turning** it off and see if that works.
10 I'll **try to get** an A in my exam.

a) attempt something you may or may not be able to do
b) wish you hadn't done something in the past
c) not remember something you have to do
d) stop so that you can then do something else
e) have a memory of something
f) feel bad about something you have to tell someone
g) not have a memory of something
h) do something to see what result it will have
i) stop an action or a habit
j) not forget something you have to do

B Choose the correct options to complete these sentences.

1 We regret *to inform* / *informing* you that your package has been lost.
2 I'm going to stop *to drive* / *driving* to work and will take the bus instead.
3 Chris remembered *to meet* / *meeting* the man before, but he couldn't remember his name.
4 They forgot *to reply* / *replying* to the invitation, and now it's too late.
5 I'll try *to fix* / *fixing* your car for you if you'd like.
6 I must remember *to buy* / *buying* a birthday card for Pete today.
7 Hannah regrets *to eat* / *eating* so much cake because now she feels sick.
8 If you want to get in shape, why don't you try *to swim* / *swimming*?
9 I'll never forget *to see* / *seeing* the Eiffel Tower for the first time.
10 Lara stopped *to get* / *getting* some gas for her car on her way home.

WATCH OUT!

(✗) I forgot handing in my assignment this morning.

(✓) _____

_____

A Read the article about how camera phones are affecting photography. Do the photographers who were interviewed for the article think that the changes are having a positive or a negative effect on photography?

1   Antonio Olmos   *positive / negative*
2   Eamonn McCabe   *positive / negative*
3   Nick Knight   *positive / negative*

B Choose the correct definitions of these phrases.

1   make someone redundant (lines 10–11)
    a) make somebody irrelevant
    b) make somebody angry
2   the scrap heap (line 12)
    a) place where things are recycled
    b) people or things who are no longer useful
3   become obsolete (lines 16–17)
    a) no longer used
    b) come back into fashion
4   revolution in (line 18)
    a) overthrow of the government
    b) drastic change in ways of thinking
5   blow it up (line 26)
    a) make something bigger
    b) make something explode

6   a scattergun approach (to photography) (line 35)
    a) take as many pictures as possible and hope that a few of them will be good
    b) take pictures of people using guns
7   of choice (line 48)
    a) generally preferred
    b) a mixture of
8   be engaged by (line 58)
    a) promise to marry
    b) be interested in

C Choose paragraphs A–E to answer the questions. You may use each paragraph more than once.

Which paragraph(s) ...		
discusses methods of training photographers?	1	
mention how photography has become more accessible for everyone?	2	
talks about how people are taking pictures rather than exiencing events?	3	
suggests that taking a lot of pictures means that you always end up with a few good pictures?	4	
compare the current situation in photography to something that happened in the past?	5	
discuss the quality of iPhone images?	6	
compare digital images to prints?	7	
states that photographers are no longer necessary?	8	

D Write an opinion essay of about 300 words with the title, "There have never been so many pictures taken, but photography is dying." Do you agree?

The death of photography:
Are camera phones destroying an art form?

From presidential selfies to never-ending Instagram feeds, the world is now drowning in images. Celebrated photographers discuss the impact of this on their craft.

A "It's really weird," says 50-year-old award-winning Mexican photographer Antonio Olmos. "Photography has never been so popular, but it's getting destroyed. There have never been so many pictures taken, but photography is dying.
5   People taking pictures of their food in a restaurant instead of eating it. People taking pictures of the Mona Lisa instead of looking at it. I think the iPhone is taking people away from their experiences." But what does Olmos mean by saying photography is dying? He argues that in the 1850s the rise of
10   photography **made many painters**, who had previously made nice livings from painting family portraits, **redundant**. Now it's the turn of professional photographers to join **the scrap heap**. "Photographers are getting destroyed by the rise of iPhones. Increasingly we don't need photographers—we can do just as
15   well ourselves."

B But doesn't that mean that some photographers are **becoming obsolete**, rather than that photography itself is dying? Isn't what we're witnessing a **revolution** in photography, thanks to digital technology, that makes it more democratic? "In one
20   sense yes," says Olmos. "I used to be sent on assignment to Iraq, Afghanistan—partly because there weren't any local photographers. Now thanks to digital technology, there are locals taking images at least as good as I can." But there's a stronger reason that makes Olmos argue photography is dying.
25   "The iPhone has a poor-quality lens. You can take a beautiful picture on the iPhone and **blow it up** for a print and it looks terrible." But who needs prints in a paper-free world? "For me the print is the ultimate expression of photography," he retorts. "When I do street photography courses, I get people to print
30   pictures—often for the first time. The idea is to slow them down, to make them make—not just take—pictures."

C *Guardian* photographer Eamonn McCabe agrees: "I think there's a depth to a print you don't get with digital." Furthermore, he thinks that digital photography is lazy. Why? Because "it's **a scattergun approach**. You snap 35 away thinking, 'One of these shots will work,' rather than concentrate on capturing the image." McCabe used to take two rolls of 24 exposures on a typical assignment. "Now I can shoot 1,000 pictures in one of these sessions on digital. I don't think photography's dead, it's just become 40 lazy. People are taking lots of pictures, but nobody's looking at them."

D For a more positive sense of what digital and camera phone technology has done to photography, I speak to Nick Knight, the British fashion photographer who's 45 just done two big assignments entirely on iPhone. "I work frequently on the iPhone. It's almost become my camera **of choice**." Indeed, Knight reckons that the current revolution in photography is as radical as what happened in the 1960s when fashion photographer David 50 Bailey got rid of his tripod and started using a handheld camera. "It gave him freedom and changed artistically what photography was. The same is true for me with the iPhone." But what about the poor-quality iPhone lens? "Who cares? The image isn't sharp? Big deal! One of my 55 favorite photographers is Robert Capa, whose pictures are a bit blurry sometimes—I love them because he's captured a moment." What Knight **is** also **engaged by** is how photography has become truly democratic. "When I was a kid there was just one camera per family, if that. 60 Now everybody has one and uses it all the time. That's great." But why? Knight has been researching images of punk bands lately. "There are hardly any images, and all of them are from on stage. Compare that with now—at a Kanye West gig you see a sea of cameras, and there's a 65 database of images."

E But doesn't this democratization of the medium threaten established photographers? Not necessarily. "I'll survive in this profession because I have skills," says Olmos. "I'm a storyteller in images; my compositions are better 70 than most people's. Just because you've got a microprocessor in your computer doesn't make you a writer. And just because you've got an Instagram app on your phone, you aren't a great photographer." 75

Adapted from an article that appeared in The Guardian.
http://www.theguardian.com/
artanddesign/2013/dec/13/death-of-
photography-camera-phones

UNIT 12 BRIGHT LIGHTS, BIG CITY

1 GRAMMAR: connectors of contrast

A 🎧 **27 Listen and complete the sentences.**

1. ☐ Rio was great _____ we didn't get to visit Sugarloaf Mountain.
2. ☐ I love traveling for pleasure _____ I really don't enjoy business travel.
3. ☐ _____ it was very crowded we enjoyed visiting the Louvre Museum in Paris.
4. ☐ London was a lot of fun _____ that it rained almost every day.
5. ☐ We decided to go to Shanghai _____ not speaking any Chinese.
6. ☐ Things have cost a little more than we'd expected. _____ we've had a fantastic vacation.

B Check the sentences in Exercise A that have correct punctuation. Correct the incorrect sentences.

C Complete the text with the correct connectors of contrast. Sometimes more than one answer is possible. You may use the connectors more than once.

| although | despite | even though | however | in spite of | nevertheless |

WATCH OUT!

⊗ Despite that we arrived an hour late, my flight to Chicago was very nice.

⊘ _____
_____
_____

NORTH VIETNAM—HANOI
Introducing Hanoi   ASIA

Hanoi walking tour, day 1: The Old Quarter

(1) _____ the noise and the pollution, Vietnam's capital city is a wonderful place to visit. In fact, it's worth visiting for the food alone! (2) _____, you can do more than just eat in this great city. (3) _____ you probably don't speak Vietnamese, it is easy to visit and enjoy many sights. The best place to start your day is in the Old Quarter. The market stalls open for breakfast at around 6 a.m. (4) _____ you may not be used to having soup for breakfast, you should try the typical Vietnamese breakfast of pho—noodle soup flavored with meat. (5) _____, if that doesn't sound good to you, then you can always get some delicious French bread. After breakfast, start your shopping on Lo Su Street. (6) _____ the fact that the narrow street is filled with motorbikes and crowds of people, it's a wonderful place to experience the real Vietnam. And (7) _____ you may not need anything new, you'll probably find a lot of things you want to buy. (8) _____, remember that it all has to fit in your suitcase!

2 VOCABULARY: formal letters

Complete the phrases with the words from the box. Then match the phrases (1–6) with the correct functions (a–f).

| concerning | Dear | disappointed | Furthermore | hearing | Sincerely |

1. We were very _____ with …
2. _____ Sir/Madam:
3. First of all, … _____, … Finally, …
4. I look forward to _____ from you.
5. I am writing _____ …
6. _____, Mrs. E.P. Ruskin

a) open a letter
b) say why you're writing
c) say that you didn't like something
d) list your main complaints
e) ask the person to reply
f) close your letter

3 WRITING: a letter of complaint

A Number the parts of the letter in the correct order.

A ☐ For these reasons, I request a full refund of the cost of the tour. I'm enclosing the tickets and a copy of my receipt for $70 as proof of payment.

B ☐ First of all, although your website says that the tour goes to the harbor, one of the city's main attractions, we did not go there. Instead we stopped at City Hall, which was a huge disappointment. Furthermore, we were supposed to stop for pictures, but the driver didn't stop. Finally, in spite of the fact that your website said the tour includes a three-course lunch, we weren't served lunch at all—only a bottle of water!

C ☐ Dear Sir/Madam:

D ☐ Sincerely,
　　　Joseph May

E ☐ I am writing concerning your river boat trip that my mother and I took last Saturday. We chose your tour, despite the high price, because it looked very pleasant on your website and was supposed to include all of the main city attractions. However, we were very disappointed with it for a number of reasons.

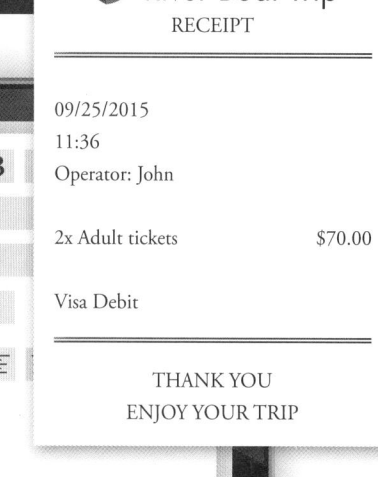

River Boat Trip
RECEIPT

09/25/2015
11:36
Operator: John

2x Adult tickets $70.00

Visa Debit

THANK YOU
ENJOY YOUR TRIP

River Boat Trip
River Boat Trip
TICKET NO: 15864
Friday
September 25, 2015
Time of issue: 11:36:12
TICKET TYPE: Adult

TICKET NO: 15864

B Match paragraphs A, B and E with their main purpose.

Paragraph A	**a)**	the writer gives details of what he doesn't like
Paragraph B	**b)**	the writer states what he wants
Paragraph E	**c)**	the writer says he's writing to complain

C Complete the letter of complaint with the phrases from the box.

> Dear Sir/Madam   Finally   First of all   For these reasons   Furthermore   I am writing concerning
> I enclose   I look forward to hearing from you   Sincerely   we were very disappointed with it

(1) ＿＿＿＿＿＿,
(2) ＿＿＿＿＿＿ my stay in your eco-lodge last month. My husband and I booked a room in your lodge, despite the high price, because it looked like a peaceful location with luxury comforts. However, **(3)** ＿＿＿＿＿＿ for a number of reasons.
(4) ＿＿＿＿＿＿, although your website clearly shows a picture of a swimming pool with people swimming in it, the pool had no water in it, so we couldn't swim. **(5)** ＿＿＿＿＿＿, the food you served was very basic, but the website says you serve high-quality gourmet food. Also, in spite of the fact that you're supposed to be an eco-lodge, we ate every meal on paper plates and used disposable plastic cups and cutlery. **(6)** ＿＿＿＿＿＿, even though your website described your rooms as "airy tree-house accommodations," our room was a small, dark building on the ground.
(7) ＿＿＿＿＿＿, I believe you should refund 75% of the cost of our stay. **(8)** ＿＿＿＿＿＿ some pictures of the empty pool, the dark room, and one basic meal, and a copy of our receipt. **(9)** ＿＿＿＿＿＿.
(10) ＿＿＿＿＿＿,
Mrs. E.P. Ruskin

4 VOCABULARY: describing places

A Put the letters into the correct order to make words used to describe places.

1 redat _____
2 taher _____
3 wevis _____
4 eylal _____

5 theagier _____
6 laglive _____
7 eist _____
8 meltentest _____

B Complete the text with the correct form of the words from Exercise A.

Jamestown
The first town of the Americas

Established in 1607, Jamestown was the first permanent **(1)** _____ of English people in the Americas. It was named in honor of King James I of England, and became the first capital of the Colony of Virginia. The settlers chose the **(2)** _____ because of its clear **(3)** _____ up and down the James River. However, the land was swampy and unsuitable for farming. In the first year, approximately half of the English colonists died of disease and famine. The others depended on **(4)** _____ with the local Native Americans for food. Eventually, the colonists grew their own food and Jamestown increased in size from a small **(5)** _____ to a bustling port town with hundreds of residents, including women and children. There were at least 100 buildings and more than a mile of streets and **(6)** _____. However, over time the town began to decline and the colonial capital was moved to Williamsburg. A few buildings in Jamestown still survive today, and it is a popular destination for tourists who want to experience the country's colonial history and **(7)** _____. The **(8)** _____ of the settlement was the beautiful Jamestown Church, which was first built in 1639 and partly restored in 1907.

5 LISTENING: rapid speech

A 🎧 28 Listen and choose the correct options to complete the sentences.

1 Sarah and Daniel are talking mostly about *plans for the future* / *recent experiences*.
2 Sarah talks mostly about *work* / *travel*.
3 Sarah mentions *members of her family* / *her boyfriend* several times.
4 Sarah and Daniel discuss a local *store* / *library*.

B Listen again. Answer the questions.

1 What country is Sarah going to visit? _____
2 What's she especially interested in? _____
3 What part of the city do Sarah's relatives live in? _____
4 What does she plan on learning while she's there? _____
5 What are Daniel's plans for the summer? _____
6 What does Sarah suggest to Daniel? _____

6 GRAMMAR: ways of talking about the future

A Match (1–4) with (a–d) to make complete sentences.

1   Use *may*, *might*, or *will*

2   Use *going to*

3   Use the present progressive

4   Use the future progressive

a)   to talk about things that will be happening at a particular time in the future.

b)   to make predictions about the future and talk about intentions.

c)   to talk about arrangements and fixed plans.

d)   to make predictions about the future.

B Choose the best options to complete the text.

America's lost cities of the future

We're fascinated by great lost cities like Peru's Machu Picchu, which was the religious heart of the great Inca Empire. We're equally fascinated by the reasons for their ruin. Often, scientists can only guess what turned the great settlements of the past into today's archeological sites. But some experts believe America's great cities of today **(1)** *may be* / *are being* the ruined cities of tomorrow, and the causes will be clear.

One American city, New Orleans, was nearly destroyed in 2005's tragic Hurricane Katrina. Even as residents rebuild, many say they have a firm plan in case another hurricane strikes: they **(2)** *might leave* / *are leaving* forever. Detroit, once a great city at the heart of the U.S. automobile trade, is already battling becoming a ghost town. Due to the collapse of the manufacturing industry in the city, almost half of the population has left and **(3)** *isn't* / *won't* planning to return. As a result, the city has had to destroy thousands of abandoned buildings. If things don't improve, the city **(4)** *is destroying* / *will be destroying* even more neighborhoods in the future and returning the land to nature.

Meanwhile, other American cities face serious threats in the future. Atlanta, once a native American village, is currently one of the country's fastest growing cities. But global warming **(5)** *may turn* / *will be turning* it into a ghost town. The problem? There isn't a large source of water near the city. If there's a drought, or the nearby river runs dry, there **(6)** *is being* / *is going to be* a serious problem. However, if sea levels rise, it's certain that Miami, about 650 miles south of Atlanta, **(7)** *will have* / *is having* the opposite problem: too much water. The city is right at sea level, and if the oceans continue to rise, Miami **(8)** *is going to be* / *is being* completely under water.

WATCH OUT!

☒ By the time this concert ends, the trains and buses won't run.

☑ _____
_____
_____

Information source: http://scribol.com/science/five-lost-cities-of-the-future

skillsStudio

A Match the headlines (1–4) with the pictures (A–D).

1 U.S. Embassy: Beijing air quality is "crazy bad" __

2 UN report says urban population to hit 5 billion by 2030 __

3 Global warming may lead to wild bears in New York in 30 years __

4 *Why we should be worried about running out of oil* __

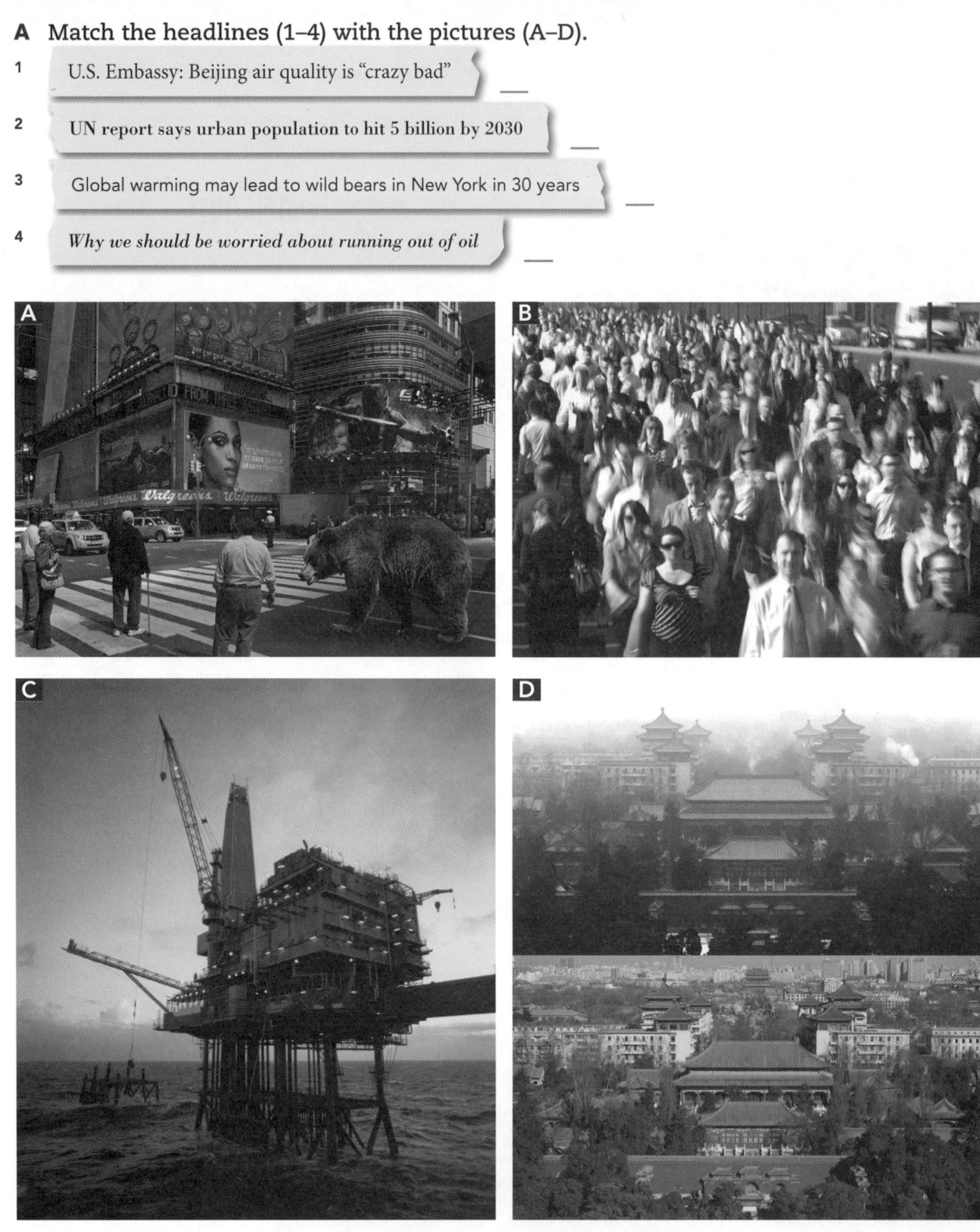

B Which problems match each headline in Exercise A? Write the correct number(s).

__ limited resources   __ overcrowding   __ climate change   __ pollution

C 🎧 29 Listen to a student give a presentation about cities of the future.
Check the problems she says cities will have to solve by 2050.

☐ limited resources   ☐ overcrowding   ☐ climate change   ☐ pollution

D Listen again. Choose the correct answer.

1 A *dome* is a kind of …
   a) fan.   b) vehicle.   c) artificial cloud.   d) roof.

2 In the presentation, the word *address* means …
   a) deal with.   b) speak about.   c) a location.   d) a formal speech.

3 The student thinks cities of the future will have cleaner air because …
   a) there will be less traffic.
   b) cars will use better gasoline.
   c) everyone will be driving electric cars.
   d) we will run out of oil to pollute the air with.

4 Why does the student mention traffic?
   a) to explain why pollution will increase in 2050
   b) to make a joke
   c) to give a reason why electric cars are better
   d) to consider an opposing argument

5 Why does the student think underwater cities might be possible?
   a) Because people in the U.S. Navy have lived underwater since the 1960s.
   b) Because science fiction writers have shown that the idea could work.
   c) Because a new city is already being built underwater right now.
   d) Because there have already been successful experiments in underwater living.

E Listen again. Check the statements that the student would probably agree with.

1 ☐ Scientists in the 1970s correctly predicted the problems cities would face.
2 ☐ Not every city today is perfect.
3 ☐ Cars are not the most important cause of air pollution.
4 ☐ There is enough oil on the planet to last for hundreds of years.
5 ☐ There is probably no way to reduce the population of cities.
6 ☐ It would be very pleasant to live on the moon.

F How do you think the place where you live will be different in 2050? Write a presentation of about 200 words. Think of two problems your area faces. For each problem, describe the issue and explain how it may be solved in your area by 2050.

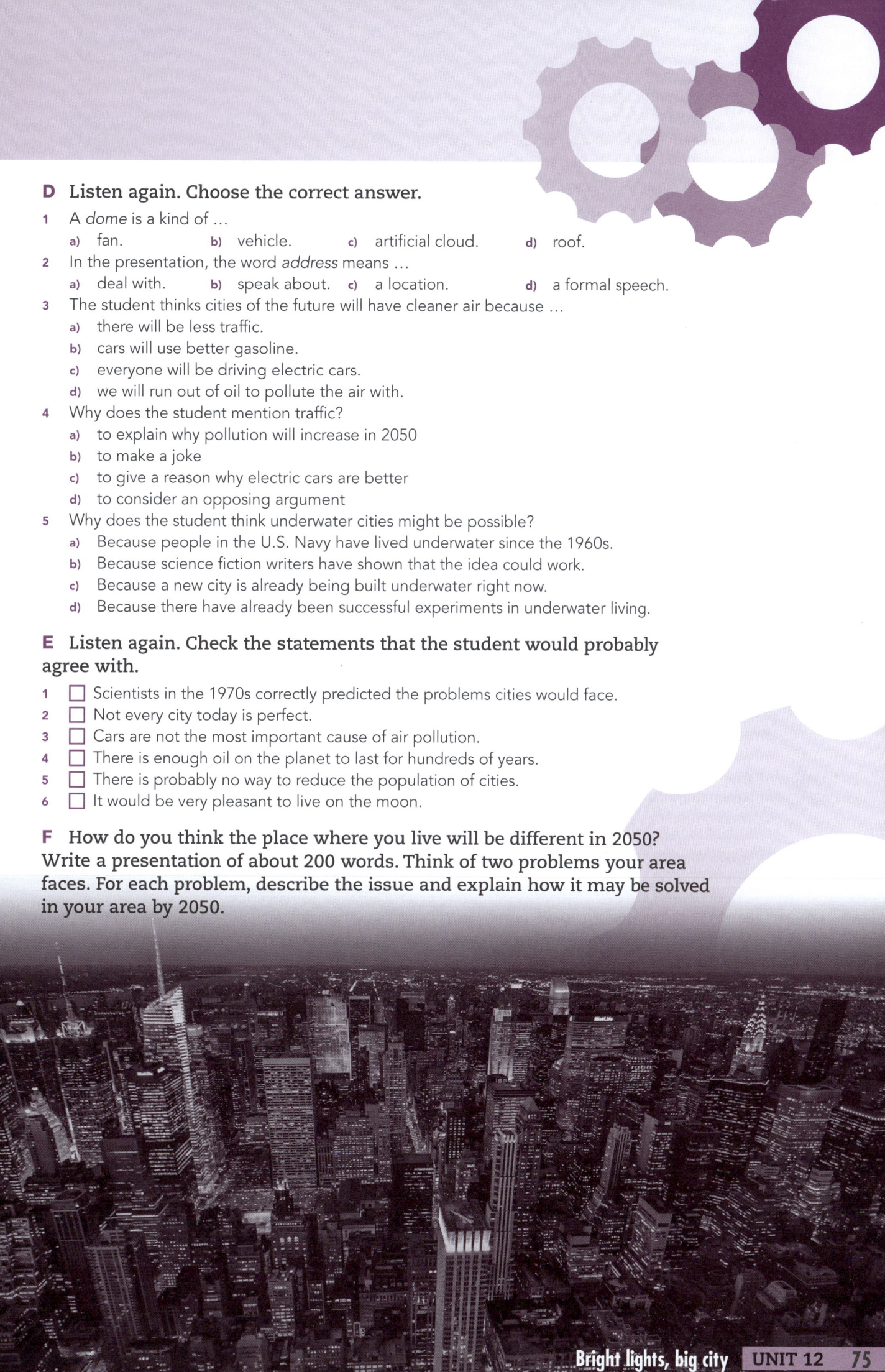

Audio script

Track 01

Matt:

Wow, that's a tough question! I think when I was younger, my friends really shaped who I was, so the social group I was part of was very important. Also I had a lot of big life goals back then. I wanted to be a musician, so music was my life and really influenced my identity. But things are different now. I'm a husband, and I'm a dad—that's how I see myself. So I guess family values are more important to my sense of identity now.

Yasmin:

Well, I've thought a lot about this since I came to the US for college. In the middle east, where I come from, a lot of people get a sense of identity from their family background. Not just your parents, but your grandparents and even great-grandparents show people who you are. If you come from a "good" family, your social status is higher and people treat you better. Now, I still think family is a really important factor in your identity, but it's not the only thing. The subject you study, your friends, and interests are factors too.

Track 02

Mark: Welcome to "Smart Talk." I'm your host, Mark Owens. Today we're talking to Lisa Adams, an expert on parenting who has just written a fascinating book on children and identity. Welcome, Dr. Adams.

Lisa: Thank you, Mark.

Mark: Now, I wanted to ask you about your chapter on clothing and children's identities. You have some very interesting and, uh, unusual ideas here.

Lisa: Yes. A lot of parents don't want to buy their children cool clothes or designer brands, because they think it will have a negative effect on their sense of identity.

Mark: And you disagree with that idea.

Lisa: Uh, yes and no. I mean, a child's identity should not be based on fashion. But at the same time, fashionable clothes make people look good, and if people look good, they feel good—even children. And kids need to be accepted by their social group. So I think it is good to buy cool clothes for your children, even when they're three or four years old.

Mark: I'm sorry, but I just don't think that's true. First of all, I think it's more important that children are comfortable and can run around and climb trees without worrying about what they look like, or damaging their expensive designer clothes. But more importantly, children shouldn't be worrying about their sense of style and social status, especially three-year-olds. It teaches them the wrong values, doesn't it?

Lisa: I'm afraid I can't agree. I think children have the right to wear designer clothes if their parents have enough money. I don't mean that children should have designer stuff worth two million dollars! But they have the right to look cool, if they want to.

Mark: In a sense, you're right: if the parents have a lot of money, why shouldn't they spend it on their kids' clothes? But I think it puts a lot of pressure on moms and dads to spend money that they don't necessarily have, so their children look cool.

Lisa: Well, yes, to a certain extent, but you know, there are non-designer brands that make cool kids' clothes.

Mark: Well, uh, that's true, but I just think that children should develop a sense of identity based on who they are, not what they wear.

Lisa: I couldn't agree more. But it's still important to look good at the same time, isn't it?

UNIT 2
Track 03

1   The thing about globalization is how dependent we all are on one another economically. I mean, if there's some sort of natural disaster or something in one part of the world, then it'll affect the markets there. Then in the following days, you know, we'll feel the ripple effects of that in stock markets across the world. If prices fall dramatically in one country, then they are going to, like, crash everywhere.

2   The other night I called my insurance company in New York because my roof started to leak during a storm. I thought I was speaking to someone in the US, but then, well, I realized I was talking to a woman in *India*. She was, like, helping me from the other side of the world. She was great. The best thing was that even though it was the middle of the night in the US, I could still talk to someone because, you know, because of the time difference. It meant that the call center was open and I could get it all taken care of right away.

3 Recently my neighbors bought a sofa from a local store. The sofa was made overseas somewhere, but they were happy, you know, because it was really comfortable. Then they started getting these, like, weird burns on their legs. The doctors couldn't find the problem. Eventually the local store announced that there was a dangerous chemical in the sofa and my neighbors got their money back. But that's not good enough. I mean, globalization is fine, but if we buy and sell things around the world, we should all have the same standards.

4 I think globalization's cool. I love using social networking sites because, well, it kind of means that I have friends all over the world now. I have, like, 500 friends. It's awesome. I mean, they send me pictures, music, videos—all kinds of stuff from their countries—and, you know, I send them things from my country, too. It's amazing.

Track 04

1 The thing about globalization is how dependent we all are on one another economically. I mean, if there's some sort of natural disaster or something in one part of the world, then it'll affect the markets there. Then in the following days, you know, we'll feel the ripple effects of that in stock markets across the world. If prices fall dramatically in one country, then they are going to, like, crash everywhere.

2 The other night I called my insurance company in New York because my roof started to leak during a storm. I thought I was speaking to someone in the US, but then, well, I realized I was talking to a woman in *India*. She was, like, helping me from the other side of the world. She was great. The best thing was that even though it was the middle of the night in the US, I could still talk to someone because, you know, because of the time difference. It meant that the call center was open and I could get it all taken care of right away.

3 Recently my neighbors bought a sofa from a local store. The sofa was made overseas somewhere, but they were happy, you know, because it was really comfortable. Then they started getting these, like, weird burns on their legs. The doctors couldn't find the problem. Eventually the local store announced that there was a dangerous chemical in the sofa and my neighbors got their money back. But that's not good enough. I mean, globalization is fine, but if we buy and sell things around the world, we should all have the same standards.

Track 05

4 I think globalization's cool. I love using social networking sites because, well, it kind of means that I have friends all over the world now. I have, like, 500 friends. It's awesome. I mean, they send me pictures, music, videos—all kinds of stuff from their countries—and, you know, I send them things from my country, too. It's amazing.

Track 06

1 support
2 promote
3 campaign
4 generate
5 value
6 sustain
7 participate
8 boost

Track 07

John: And now it's time for our weekly feature, *Let's Talk Travel*. And joining me in the studio today is Scott Williams, author of a brand new book called *Sustainable Travel*. He's here to speak to us about ethical tourism. Welcome to the show, Scott.

Scott: Thanks for inviting me, John. It's great to be here.

John: So, Scott, tell us, what is an ethical tourist exactly?

Scott: Well, an ethical tourist is a traveler who does everything possible to make sure that the impact that they have on the local environment, culture, and people of the country that they are visiting is positive and not negative.

John: Oh, OK. I see. So how can countries be affected negatively by tourism?

Scott: Well, for a start, tourism can be harmful to the environment. With globalization, there are more airplanes flying around the planet than ever before, which means increased carbon emissions. I read somewhere that there are something like 93,000 flights every day!

John: Wow, that's certainly a lot of carbon in the air …

Scott: It is. And by now, we all know the dangers of global warming … But it's not just that. Tourists sometimes ruin some of the most beautiful and remote areas of the world because they leave trash behind them, which can be really hard to get rid of. And the demands of tourism can also sometimes threaten the limited natural resources of an area, such as water. For example, an average-sized golf course can use more than half a million gallons of water EVERY SINGLE DAY. Some areas just don't have enough water to sustain that sort of demand.

John: Yes, I see … And are there any other problems that can be caused by tourism?

Scott: Oh, definitely. Tourism can sometimes harm local communities.

John: Really? That surprises me. Why is that? I mean, surely tourism is good for local communities, isn't it? It generates jobs and boosts the local economy. A lot of people depend on the tourism trade, don't they?

Scott: Yes, that's true. But, unfortunately, the tourism market is often dominated by multinational companies and, in some places, regional businesses just can't compete with the prices. And what's more, sometimes local people are forced to leave their homes to make way for tourism developments …

John: That's awful. So, what can we do about it? How can we all become ethical tourists?

Scott: Well, there are all kinds of things we can do. For a start, wherever possible, we should use ethical transportation—like the train, boat, or even bike.

John: I hear what you're saying, Scott. But are you being realistic? It's not always possible to do that, is it? For example most people only have a few days' vacation a year—if they want to visit Vietnam, they don't have time to take a boat!

Scott: No, that's true. But there are other ways that we can play a role in helping the environment, for example, we can leave any excess packaging at home. Remember that some countries don't have the waste facilities to deal with our trash.

John: Yes, that's a good idea. What else can we do?

Scott: Well, make sure you find out about the ethics of your tour operator before you hand over your money. An ethical company will be more than willing to share information about subjects such as whether they pay their local employees a fair wage, for example. Just be conscious of the fact that some operators care more about making money than helping local people.

John: I'm sorry, but I'm going to have to stop you there, Scott, because we're running out of time. Thank you so much for coming in to talk to us today.

UNIT 3
Track 08

1

A: Hey, have you read the new Stephen King novel?

B: No, it's not really my thing.

A: You should read it. It's really creepy. I couldn't put it down!

2

A: Muhammad Ali is one of the greatest people ever.

B: Do you really think so? What about Gandhi and Martin Luther King? As great as them?

3

A: I think it's horrible that so many young people just want to be famous.

B: What do you mean?

4

A: I think friendship must be really hard for famous people.

B: No way! Famous people all have lots of friends. Other famous people!

5

A: I don't know why Kanye West got together with Kim Kardashian. He's so talented, but she … well, you know.

B: So you're saying you don't think she has talent?

6

A: Anyone can break a world record and become famous.

B: Oh, yeah, right. So you're going to run a marathon in two hours and the world will know your name?

Track 09

1

A: Hey, have you read the new Stephen King novel?

B: No, it's not really my thing.

A: You should read it. It's really creepy. I couldn't put it down!

B: Maybe I'm not making myself clear. I don't read horror books at all. They're too scary for me!

2

A: Muhammad Ali is one of the greatest people ever.

B: Do you really think so? What about Gandhi and Martin Luther King? As great as them?

A: Well, perhaps I should rephrase that—he's one of the greatest athletes ever.

3

A: I think it's horrible that so many young people just want to be famous.

B: What do you mean?

A: Talent used to come first, put it that way. In the past, kids wanted to be famous for being good at something. Now they just want fame!

4

A: I think friendship must be really hard for famous people.

B: No way! Famous people all have lots of friends. Other famous people!

A: What I'm trying to say is, fame makes it hard for famous people to maintain relationships with non-celebrities because their lives are so different.

5

A: I don't know why Kanye West got together with Kim Kardashian. He's so talented, but she … well, you know.

B: So you're saying you don't think she has talent?

A: Actually, that's not what I meant. She's got some talent. She's good at promoting herself. But he's just so much more talented.

6

A: Anyone can break a world record and become famous.

B: Oh, yeah, right. So you're going to run a marathon in two hours and the world will know your name?

A: Well, what I meant was, you can come up with your own idea, like sitting in a tree for the longest time or something, and then do it, and you get famous!

UNIT 4

Track 10

Australia is officially the happiest country in the world for the fourth year running. That's according to the Better Life Index, which is put together each year by the Organization for Economic Cooperation and Development (OECD). In general, it's not easy to measure well-being. As a result, OECD ranks their 36 member countries according to 11 different criteria. They consider things that affect material living conditions, including housing, income, and jobs. In addition, they look at features that influence the quality of life—these are community, environment, education, civic engagement, health, safety, life satisfaction, and work-life balance.

So far, 60,000 people have taken part in the research, sharing their views about each of these areas. What's more, people are able to state which criteria are most important to them. To a great extent, the most important factor for people's happiness is life satisfaction, closely followed by health and education.

Scandinavia dominates the top five with Norway, Sweden, and Denmark at numbers 2, 3, and 4 respectively. Furthermore, Finland comes in at number 8. On the other hand, at the other end of the list is Greece, whose citizens have the lowest life satisfaction, and as a consequence they come in at number 34. That said, it's not all bad news. Greece reports above average health and quality of environment. Mexico is in 35th place—on the whole there is a high level of life satisfaction, but safety is a significant issue. Turkey ranks poorly in income and housing areas, and consequently, it comes in at 36th place. Nevertheless, Turkey is praised for improving the quality of life for citizens over the last 20 years.

Track 11

1. pessimistic
2. depressed
3. state of well-being
4. optimistic
5. in a good mood
6. distracted
7. emotions
8. focused

Track 12

Susie: Hey, Grandpa, I'm reading this article about the ages when people are happiest.

Ron: Really? And when are people happiest?

Susie: Well, according to a recent report our happiness peaks twice in our lives. The first peak is when we're 23. I'm almost 24! Does that mean it's all downhill from here? That's depressing. Do you agree with that? Were you happiest at 23?

Ron: Well, I was very happy at that age, yes. At 23 you're young and optimistic about life. You have a lot of expectations about what lies ahead. In addition, you don't have any of the responsibilities or worries that you have later in life. And life is fun and full of possibility.

Susie: Well, I suppose I'd better make the most of it and appreciate every moment then! Anyway, the article says that when you're 23, you overestimate your future life satisfaction by an average of about 10%. Then over the next few decades, you begin to feel more and more disappointed about life until you hit a low point in your mid 50s.

Ron: Why is that? What is it about your mid 50s that's so bad?

Susie: It says that's the age when you have the strongest feeling of regret because you realize that the dreams you had when you were younger aren't going to come true.

Ron: Hmm, I don't agree with that at all. When you're in your 50s, there's still time to pursue your dreams.

Susie: Oh, yes. That's right. You had a career change at about that stage of your life, didn't you?

Ron: Yes, I quit my job in sales when I was 53 and retrained as a yoga instructor. It was the best move I ever made—I may not have been as wealthy after that, but at least I had a job that I enjoyed. And I was much, much more content than I had ever been before. So, what does it say about after the age of 55?

Susie: Well, interestingly, that's when satisfaction levels start to rise again as you accept the disappointments in your life. Then, your state of well-being peaks when you reach the age of 69.

Ron: Hmm, why 69, I wonder?

Susie: Well, it says that 68 year-olds underestimate their future happiness by 4.5%, so maybe that's why. As you get older, you have lower expectations about life, so you have fewer disappointments, and so consequently, you feel more content.

Ron: Now, that I do agree with. As you get older, your expectations do change. So, what happens after 69?

Susie: Hmm. It says satisfaction levels decline after 75 …

Ron: Well, bearing in mind that I'm almost 80, that hasn't put me in a good mood! I hate to say it but, on the whole, I agree with that. I get frustrated these days that I can't do what I used to in spite of all the yoga I've done over the years! I'd be interested to know more about that report though. Do you know how many people they spoke to and what backgrounds they came from? Because I think it's very hard to generalize about happiness.

Susie: Hang on, it says here somewhere … oh, yes. Here it is. It was based on German data from more than 23,161 individuals, between the ages of 17 and 85. And they spoke to people from east and west Germany, and the results that they got were similar in spite of the economic and cultural differences between the two regions.

Ron: Hmm, that's interesting. Maybe there is something to it then …

UNIT 5

Track 13

A: Should we order a bottle of water for the table?

B: Maybe. Uh, how much does one cost?

A: Let's see. They range from five to ten dollars.

B: Five dollars? It would have to be a big bottle to make it worth that much.

A: It's no more expensive than soda. And it tastes better than tap water.

B: Really? I bet if tap water was put up against bottled water in a taste test you wouldn't be able to tell the difference!

A: Sure I would!

B: Well, maybe … but for me it's as much about the environment as it is the price. Those plastic bottles are bad for the planet. They really shouldn't market it as something clean and healthy, you know?

A: But it makes me feel healthy!

B: But bottled water IS bad for the environment, AND it's too expensive.

A: OK, OK! Let's just get tap water!

Track 14

Kirsten: Look at this. What can we do to raise awareness about water pollution?

Tim: We could try collecting some trash from the river and displaying it.

Kirsten: I like that idea! I'd suggest putting it on display by the river.

Tim: Maybe, but the trash might fall into the river again. What about displaying it somewhere indoors? There's always the school.

Jess: No, not the school. Since adult shoppers throw most of the trash in the river, let's focus on them. Have you considered giving the shopping mall a try?

Tim: Nice idea, but I don't think the mall would accept the trash. Hey, what if we take pictures of the trash instead? We could display pictures in the mall.

Jess: Or another option would be to hand out leaflets …

UNIT 6

Track 15

1

Interviewer: Hello, I'm doing a survey about weddings. I wonder if you could spare a moment to share your views on the subject. Do you think weddings are an important ritual in society?

Speaker 1: Well, I guess weddings are important, but they cost so much money these days. People are under a lot of pressure to organize the perfect event. You've got the new clothes, the venue, the food, the flowers, not to mention the honeymoon. I mean, it can end up costing thousands of dollars. And sometimes it's the young couple that has to pay for it all. Quite frankly, I think that young people have better things to spend their money on, like saving to buy a house. After all, a wedding only lasts for one day, but a house lasts a lifetime, right?

2

Speaker 2: Yes, definitely. I love going to weddings. They're just wonderful. Everyone wears amazing clothes, too. It's the one day of your life when you get to be a star with all of your friends and family. The other thing is—and I know this is really old-fashioned—but I think it's important for people to be serious about being together, you know? It's a big step and it's important to mark the occasion.

3

Speaker 3: Well, I have to confess that I don't really like going to traditional weddings! I mean, weddings are an important ritual and all, but I just find them boring sometimes. When I was young, weddings were all the same. The man wore a dark suit. The woman wore a white dress. But nowadays, you can have it any way you want and you have so much more choice. So a wedding is important not because it's traditional, but because you can do it your own way—barefoot at the beach, jumping out of an airplane— anything goes.

4

Speaker 4: Well, getting married is important, but I don't think the wedding ceremony part of it is that important. I believe that people are just wasting their money—and mine! I went to five weddings last year and I spent a fortune on presents. I'm tired of going to weddings now. You know, I'm all for love, and I'm happily married myself, but it's just crazy to spend tens of thousands of dollars on one party.

Track 16

1 freshman
2 initiation
3 mascot
4 high-ranking
5 ritual
6 symbolic

Track 17

1   One of the most unusual festivals in my country, Thailand, is the Monkey Buffet Festival, which is held in Lopburi. The area is full of monkeys and, once a year, the villagers hold a picnic in their honor. Over 600 monkeys enjoy grilled sausage, fresh fruit, ice cream, and other monkey treats! Monkeys are traditionally treated with respect in Thailand, but having said that, the Monkey Buffet Festival is not a tradition that dates back very far. It was started in 1989 by a local hotel owner— to be honest, I think the motivation for setting up this tradition may have been more about promoting tourism rather than honoring wildlife. It has certainly boosted tourism in the region because the festival gets bigger and better each year, pulling in lots of visitors hoping to catch sight of this unusual festivity.

2   The most unusual festival in my country is the annual Cheese-Rolling Festival, which is held every May in Gloucestershire in the west of England—basically, a large round of cheese is rolled down a hill and the competitors race down to see who can catch it. The person who catches the cheese gets to take it home! Nobody is quite sure where this tradition comes from, but it's at least 200 years old. Some think it used to be a fertility ritual to encourage a big harvest; others say it was what people used to have to do to maintain their right to use the land for their animals. But, to be honest, nowadays it's just an excuse to turn up and have a good laugh!

3   The highlight of the festival calendar in Spain for me is La Tomatina (that's L-A T-O-M-A-T-I-N-A), which is held on the last Wednesday of August every year in the town of Buñol near Valencia. It's basically the biggest food fight in the world! It's such good fun—over the course of exactly one hour, we hurl 100 tons of overripe tomatoes at each other! The festival started in about 1944 and it seems to get bigger each year. Just recently, the town has started to sell entry tickets to cover the costs of the event. I guess it's fair enough really—you can just imagine what the streets look like by the end and the fire engines have to clean up using fire hoses.

4   There's a great festival on the island of Shetland, in Scotland called Up Helly Aa. It's a fire festival to mark the end of winter where the local people dress as Vikings and parade through the town at night with torches. At the end of the parade everyone sets fire to a ship called a galley. Then the parade splits into groups and they do comedy or entertaining acts at different venues around the town. It's a fascinating spectacle to watch and the night really generates a strong feeling of community. You should definitely look it up online. It's spelled U-P, space, H-E-L-L-Y, space, A-A.

5   An unusual ritual in my country, Japan, is Konaki Sumo (that's K-O-N-A-K-I, space, S-U-M-O). What happens is two Sumo wrestlers face each other and each of them holds a baby, also facing forward. The winner is the baby who starts to cry first. And if both babies start to cry at the same time, then the winner is the one who cries the loudest. It may sound strange, but we have this old proverb, "crying babies grow fast," because we believe that the louder a baby cries the more the gods have blessed it. It's a ritual that's at least 400 years old, and it gives us a chance to be grateful for the babies' health.

UNIT 7

Track 18

Jim:	I want to paint the kitchen, and I was hoping we could talk about the colors.
Nicole:	Sure. I was thinking we might choose a neutral color, like cream.
Jim:	Oh, really? I wanted to suggest using something more exciting.
Nicole:	More exciting? Like what?
Jim:	I was wondering if we should paint it orange and red.
Nicole:	Orange and red?! I'm not sure that's the best idea. Those colors don't really work with the table and chairs.
Jim:	Yeah, I guess. Maybe cream is best, after all.

UNIT 8

Track 19

1. poverty
2. ambassador
3. philanthropic
4. humanitarian
5. refugee
6. injustice
7. underprivileged
8. foundation

Track 20

1. In today's lecture we'll be looking at the movement to eradicate poverty through market-based solutions. We'll be focusing on a pioneering company, now called Ten Thousand Villages, which began the fair-trade movement. First, a bit of background information. Ten Thousand Villages is a non-profit charitable fair-trade organization that buys the handcrafted products it sells, for example, jewelry, items for the home, toys, games, baskets, stationery, and so on, directly from the producers. And, being a fair-trade company, all of their products are bought at a fair price. The products are sold through a retail network of over seventy stores— mostly in shopping centers—and online. The company also sells a number of products to hundreds of other retailers throughout the US, and they sell directly to customers at festivals, usually hosted by community groups, churches, or colleges.

2. Now let's move on to the company's history. It all started when an American named Edna Ruth Byler visited Puerto Rico in 1946. While there, she met a number of women artisans. She was impressed with their work, but was shocked by the poverty in which they lived, and wanted to take action to help them. Following that trip, Byler started an organization called the Overseas Needlepoint and Crafts Project that bought the products for a fair price and sold them in the North American market. For the next thirty years, she worked to help artisans in developing countries—for example Cambodia, the Philippines, Uganda, and countless others— to sell their products at fair prices in the US The business became extremely successful and improved the lives of thousands of artisans and their families who had been living in poverty. Byler retired in 1979, but others continued her work.

3. Now, let's turn our attention to its more recent history. In 1996, the organization celebrated its 50th birthday. It changed its name to Ten Thousand Villages, and in 1997, it opened the first Ten Thousand Villages store: prior to that, the products had been sold to other organizations and retailers. Then in 2006, the company began selling its products online, which has proven to be a huge success. Recently, Ten Thousand Villages has been named one of the world's most ethical companies by Forbes Magazine and the Ethisphere Institute. And the company's vision continues to be that no artisan will be exploited.

   Now, I'd like to look in some detail at exactly where …

Track 21

Sophia: Welcome back, you're listening to Radio 35 *Daily Debate* with me, Sophia Peters. Next, we're going to talk about celebrity humanitarians and whether they do more harm than good. I'm joined in the studio today by two guests—journalist Paul Cunard, and Rosie Simons, who is a representative of the Kitts Humanitarian Foundation. Thank you both for joining us today.

Paul: It's a pleasure.

Rosie: Good to be here.

Sophia: OK, Paul, let's start with you—you've recently written a very passionate article called "Celebrity do-gooders do more harm than good." Tell us more.

Paul: Well, I just don't buy into the whole celebrity humanitarian thing, I'm afraid. We've all heard about celebrities doing their part for charities. But in my opinion, the only reason that celebrities get involved in charity work is to promote themselves and raise their profiles. They pretend to be helping the poor, but really they are just making themselves richer.

Sophia: Rosie, I can see you shaking your head. Would you like to join in here?

Rosie: Yes, I would. I don't think it's helpful to make such broad generalizations about people's motivations—some of these people are just trying to use their profiles to raise awareness about issues they care about.

Paul: I'm sorry, Rosie, but I think you're being a little naïve.

Rosie: No, I'm not. Just because a person is rich or famous doesn't mean they aren't allowed to feel a sense of social responsibility. Maybe they feel it even more strongly because they have so much, whereas others have so little. How can you be so sure that their intentions are bad?

Paul: Well, the facts speak for themselves. It's all about money. For example, the Live 8 concerts in 2005 turned out to be great marketing for the corporate sponsors. And the artists who generously gave their time for free got to play to the whole world and some had increased sales of up to 3,600% in the week after the concerts. Frankly, I don't think it had much to do with getting governments to make promises about global poverty.

Rosie: OK, I hear what you're saying. But the good that celebrity ambassadors can do for a charity far outweighs the negatives that you're highlighting. You can't deny that people like Angelina Jolie, George Clooney, and Bono have made an enormous contribution to humanitarian efforts. And, in my experience, charity organizations are delighted when they receive support from well-known faces because a celebrity endorsement usually raises a charity's profile, which means that they get more donations from the public.

Paul: I appreciate that, but the worrying thing is that celebrities tend to focus attention and resources on short-term, media-friendly crises, which means that we end up dealing with the symptoms rather than the causes of the problems. The media focus on the dramatic pictures of children crying and destroyed houses, without dealing with the main issues of social inequality.

Sophia: Rosie, would you like to respond to that?

Rosie: Yes, I would. I couldn't disagree more. What about Ben Affleck's Eastern Congo Initiative? That's not a short-term reaction to a crisis. He founded this initiative a few years ago and it helps to fund local Congolese-led programs to build safe and sustainable communities for the future.

Paul: I see your point, Rosie. Maybe there are a few exceptions to the rule but generally, I think we're just going to have to agree to disagree on this …

Sophia: And I'm afraid that I'm going to have to stop you there, Paul because we've run out of time. Thank you both for coming in and talking to us today. We like nothing more than a lively discussion here at *Daily Debate!*

UNIT 9
Track 22

A: Here's an interesting article. It's all about how to win at "Rock, Paper, Scissors."

B: That's ridiculous. There's no skill or strategy for that game.

A: Well, maybe. The article says many people think that winning or losing in "Rock, Paper, Scissors" is mostly about luck.

B: Exactly.

A: Let me finish. But actually, you can use strategies to win.

B: OK, like what, for example?

A: Here's one. Statistics show that players with less experience usually begin a game by playing the "rock" gesture.

B: Really? There are studies on this?

A: That's what it says. Anyway, that's why you should always start with "paper" against an inexperienced player.

B: Because your opponent is probably going to play rock, and paper beats rock.

A: Exactly.

B: That's fine, but what if my opponent already knows about that strategy?

A: Simple. You should play scissors first to beat experienced players because they'll know the tactic and will begin with paper.

B: All right, I can believe that. What else does it say?

A: It says you have a good opportunity to win if the person you're playing against makes the same gesture twice.

B: Oh, why is that?

A: Well, the other player will probably make a different gesture the third time because they think this will be more difficult to predict.

B: And isn't it?

A: Actually, no. Let's say the other person plays paper, and then paper again. The third time, they'll probably do rock or scissors.

B: Not paper.

A: Exactly. So you can play rock. You might win, you might tie, but you won't lose.

B: I never thought of that!

UNIT 10
Track 23

1 be exposed to
2 dare to
3 failure
4 freedom
5 play it safe
6 risky
7 security
8 take a chance

Track 24

Dave: Hey Mae, did you hear that they've closed off the recreation area in the park?

Mae: No, why did they do that?

Dave: Well, apparently, a boy fell off the slide and broke his arm, so I guess they must have decided that it's unsafe.

Mae: You've got to be kidding. People are just too overprotective these days.

Dave: You're right; it's kind of extreme. But I think parents just want to keep their kids safe.

Mae: Well, I think that children need to take risks in order to learn how to manage risks.

Dave: Oh, I don't know about that. If I had kids, I wouldn't want them playing in a park where somebody had broken their arm.

Mae: But accidents can happen anywhere. That kid could have fallen out of bed and broken his arm! Children learn basic survival skills through play, and if we don't let them take risks when they are young, then they won't know how to handle them when they grow up.

Dave: Hmm, you've got a point there.

Track 25

Jane: Good evening, everybody. My name is Jane Franks and I'd like to welcome you all here this evening. It is my very great honor to introduce Joe Scott, mountain climber and adventurer, who is here to talk to us about his latest expedition—climbing Mount Kangchengjunga. Let's give him a warm welcome.

Joe: Thank you, thank you very much. It's a pleasure to be here. I love talking about my passion—mountain climbing—so I was absolutely delighted to receive the invitation to come and talk to you all this evening! So, as Jane mentioned, I've recently arrived back from climbing Mount Kangchengjunga.

Now, before I start, just out of interest, let's have a quick show of hands. Who here knows anything about Mount Kangchengjunga? Oh, OK, good to see that there are a few hands up at least! But, as I thought, this is a mountain that not many people are familiar with—even though it's one of the highest in the world and one of the most dangerous to climb. So I'd like to start by telling you a little more about it. It's 28,169 feet high and it's on the border between Nepal and India. It's the third highest mountain in the world after Everest and K2, but in terms of difficulty of climbing, it's generally considered harder to climb than Everest, which is 820 feet higher, and it's just as difficult as K2, which is 40 feet higher.

My group and I went up the southwest face of the mountain at the head of the Yalung Valley. The route we took was along a snow ramp until we reached the West Ridge and then upward to the summit. The last push was really extreme and involved some very tough climbing. When we got to the top, we didn't walk on the summit itself out of respect for the local Sikkimese people who consider it to be sacred. The first team to climb the mountain (a British expedition led by Charles Evans in 1955) made a promise to the Maharaja of Sikkim that human feet would not walk on the summit when they climbed it, so we decided that we should honor this promise, too.

As I already mentioned, Kangchengjunga is one of the most dangerous mountains in the world to climb—the main risks are from avalanches and bad weather. We were very lucky that we didn't have either during our climb. Another problem is that there is no easy route to the top—whichever way you go, you have to cross some very difficult ground. And also, once you get to the top, you're not guaranteed to get back safely. Not every mountaineer has been as fortunate as we were—more than 20% of the people who have tried to climb Kangchengjunga have lost their lives.

Now, people often ask me why I risk my life to reach new heights, so I thought I'd try and answer that for you here tonight. I wouldn't describe myself as reckless or a thrill-seeker. In contrast, I am focused, disciplined. I love what I do and I have spent years of my life training for it. What I feel when I reach the summit is not the adrenalin rush that other climbers talk about, but rather a real sense of achievement and the realization of how powerful nature is. I feel truly peaceful—it's almost like meditation. Some people think that extreme sportspeople have to be risk takers. I disagree. I don't take risks—risk is all about uncertainty and about not being in control. I do everything I can to reduce the risks and would never put myself in a situation where I'm not in control.

So to finish, I would say that my climb up Mount Kangchengjunga was one of the most rewarding experiences of my life. Now I'm going to go away and plan my next adventure! Maybe it'll be K2 next! OK, does anyone have any questions …?

UNIT 11

Track 26

1 Both pictures are alike in that they are taken in New York City.

2 In Picture A, the subject of the picture is a person, while in Picture B the subject is the city.

3 In Picture A, it's daytime, whereas in Picture B it's sunset.

4 Another point of difference is the area of the city that the pictures show. One is of a bridge over the river, and the other is of a street and skyscrapers.

5 Picture A is very bright and, in contrast, Picture B is dark.

6 Both pictures are similar in that they were probably both taken by professional photographers.

7 Picture A was taken by Tuan Tuan, unlike Picture B, which was taken by Zoran Milich.

8 One similarity is that there are skyscrapers in both pictures.

UNIT 12

Track 27

1 Rio was great; however, we didn't get to visit Sugarloaf Mountain.

2 I love traveling for pleasure, but I really don't enjoy business travel.

3 Although it was very crowded, we enjoyed visiting the Louvre Museum in Paris.

4 London was a lot of fun despite the fact that it rained almost every day.

5 We decided to go to Shanghai despite not speaking any Chinese.

6 Things have cost a little more than we'd expected. Nevertheless, we've had a fantastic vacation.

Track 28

Daniel: Have you decided what you're doing this summer, Sarah?

Sarah: I'm going to China. My grandparents came from there, you know, so I'd really like to see it.

Daniel: That's so cool, Sarah! Where are you going to go?

Sarah: I'm going to go to Beijing. I still have a lot of family there.

Daniel: So do you speak any Chinese?

Sarah: Well, yeah, a little. My mom speaks Chinese really well, and she spoke it to me when I was a kid.

Daniel: I bet you'll have a great time.

Sarah: Oh, yeah. The history and the architecture there are amazing. There's the Great Wall, of course, which isn't far from the city, and there's the Forbidden City and the Summer Palace, but at the same time there are ultra-modern skyscrapers everywhere. I'm really, really into that kind of contrast. Have you ever been to Asia?

Daniel: Yeah, sort of. When my family visited Australia, our plane stopped in Japan for a day, in Tokyo. I loved it! Of course it's probably very different from Beijing.

Sarah: True. But both are big, exciting, crowded cities.

Daniel: Yeah. So where do your cousins live in Beijing?

Sarah: That's the best part. They're right in the center.

Daniel: What, you mean you're going to be living in the middle of the city?

Sarah: Yeah. My cousin's apartment is right in the cultural heart of Beijing, and it's also near lots of amazing shopping and food on this street called Wangfujing.

Daniel: That'll be great.

Sarah: Yeah, and one of my cousins has already said she wants to teach me all about Chinese cooking.

Daniel: Oh, man, you've got to come to my house and cook for me when you get back!

Sarah: I would love to cook you some Chinese food when I get back. Anyway, so what are you doing this summer?

Daniel: I'm definitely going to find a job. I just don't know where I'm going to be working.

Sarah: What kind of job?

Daniel: Anything, really.

Sarah: Hey, I know a guy who works at a little bookstore downtown. He might need someone.

Daniel: Hey, I'd work in a bookstore. It'd probably be nice and quiet, and I could do a lot of reading!

Sarah: You'd probably get free coffee, too. They have a little café in there. It's called Greenhouse Books. It's in a little alley off Main Street. I'd be happy to introduce you.

Track 29

Good morning, everyone. The topic for my presentation today is cities, specifically the *future* of cities. People have always loved to imagine what the cities of the future will be like. Back in the 1970s, for instance, after so many successful trips to space, scientists were fairly certain that by the year 2000, there would be a city on the moon, and that this would be the first step in solving the overcrowding here on Earth. And at that time, other experts who were concerned about air pollution, predicted that by the year 2008, some large cities would actually have domes over them. Obviously, those predictions weren't *completely* accurate.

Of course, it's very easy to laugh at these predictions, but the people who made them were very serious, and they were attempting to address very significant challenges like overcrowding and pollution. And, obviously, we still face those problems today. We love and celebrate the world's great cities, but at the same time we also know they have their problems: they can be incredibly polluted or extremely overcrowded—and sometimes both, unfortunately. So, even though earlier predictions have not come true, there is still an important question to answer. Will future cities solve problems like pollution and overcrowding? To address that question, I'd like to discuss some of the predictions that scientists today are making about the cities of 2050.

First, pollution. We know this is a problem in some cities, where it's sometimes dangerous just to go outside. However, some experts predict that the city of 2050 is going to have cleaner air. That's because we'll all probably be driving electric cars, which don't pollute the air like today's cars that use gasoline. Some of you may be thinking that this is another unrealistic prediction that won't come true. After all, currently there are very few electric cars on the roads and they are too expensive for most drivers, but that's going to change in the coming decades. For one thing, gasoline may be relatively affordable today, but it is going to become extremely expensive as the world's supply of oil is reduced. Then, at the same time, electric cars will become cheaper to manufacture. So we'll have more electric cars and the air will be cleaner, but there will still be terrible traffic.

Great. Now that we've discussed pollution, let's turn to another problem facing cities of the future: overcrowding. All over the world, this problem is getting worse. Some experts think that by 2030, over 5 billion of the world's people will be living in cities. So in 2050, what will cities be doing about overcrowding? To address the problem, some experts believe that we will actually be building new cities under the ocean. It sounds like science fiction, but there is already research on this idea.

In the 1960s and 70s, the US Navy's Sealab program experimented with having divers live for weeks at a time under the water. Other countries carried out similar experiments at that time. Since it certainly isn't likely that cities will become less crowded, it's very possible that we may be forced to live in cities under the ocean by 2050. In that case, I suppose we won't be driving electric cars. Maybe electric submarines, though.

Now, what about even further in the future, 100 years from now? Many experts believe that as the world's cities continue to grow, the planet will have even more limited natural resources. If this happens, people will need to build cities in space or on other planets. One place to go might be the moon. Scientists recently discovered a cave on the moon that could be the perfect place to start a settlement. How many of you would like to live there? No one? Well, maybe that city won't be overcrowded!